SIMPSON'S WILL

SIMPSON'S WILL

EDWARD A. McCOYD

NEW STREET
PUBLISHING

*To my friend Henry Pildner, Jr.,
who taught me how to write, and to my son Ed,
who made sure I hadn't forgotten.*

THE LIGHT IN THE APARTMENT was as brilliant as only a high-rise building can afford. It came from below, above and within, flooding into the rooms and around, through and off the glass and chrome of the modern furnishings. All seemed new, as if recently installed under the direction of a talented interior decorator. Nowhere were visible the more frayed but comfortable signs of prolonged occupancy.

The floors were wood and highly polished, covered here and there with Persian carpets of various sizes. As he walked quickly across them, his footfall was alternately sharp and silent, accentuating the emptiness of the rooms. He was dressed conservatively, in the manner of an urban executive. His navy blue, well-tailored suit would have been uncomfortably warm except in this temperature-controlled environment. Similar in their impractical beauty were his shoes, whose soft and supple black leather was not markedly different in appearance than the thin and slippery undersoles.

Ahead of him was an interior room. It was noticeably darker than those through which he had come, due both to its lack of sunlight and the wood paneling and shaded lighting that dominated its decor. Its most noticeable feature was a bar.

As he entered the room, he paused momentarily to let his eyes adjust to the dimness. He found the light switch, flipped it on, and then proceeded to the bar. Once there, he groped for the requirements of his mission and soon succeeded in mixing a drink, then settled into one of the new leather chairs next to the bar. He drank thoughtfully and moodily, glancing occasionally at the telephone on the table next to his chair. Finally, a decision made, he picked up the telephone and dialed.

He spoke with confidence. "Hello, this is Mr. Simpson. Let me have Mr. Johnson, please."

After a short pause, he spoke again. "Mildred, how are you? This is Mr. Simpson. Put Mr. Johnson on, will you?"

Once more he paused briefly, then his words came rapidly. "Hugh, this is Rex. I'm at home—the apartment. I left early. I haven't been getting a thing accomplished lately, and I think it would be best if I stayed out through the weekend. Maybe get away a bit, whatever. It will recharge my batteries, and I need that. No calls, no reminders. Would you cover for me tomorrow and Friday?"

Apparently receiving a favorable response, he continued the conversation long enough to mention a few matters requiring immediate attention and to ask that his secretary be notified. He thanked the other man and hung up. The task completed, he relaxed visibly and rose to refill his glass, then returned to his chair.

Several hours passed before he left the room. When he did, the apartment was dark. He hesitated, deciding whether to negotiate the darkness or return to the comforting light emanating from the room he had just left. Then, whether by design or inability to control his momentum, he quickly lurched forward into the gloom. A dozen steps were all he had managed before he reached the first small Persian rug. The rug, which had been placed directly on the bare floor, offered little resistance to his step and gave way almost immediately.

As his legs flew out from under him, he vainly tried to regain purchase with his feet. His slippery soles and alcohol-slowed reactions made that attempt comical. The alcohol would probably have been his ally, however, in relaxing him during his fall, had his head not struck the corner of a heavy glass coffee table just before he hit the floor.

The blood immediately spurted from his head and began to stain his silver hair. As he staggered to his feet, the flow increased and spread to the collar and then the front of his white shirt. Nevertheless, he felt no pain.

Resuming his journey, he eventually found his bedroom. He laid down on his bed as if he were only weary, and not injured. He closed his eyes and slept, a rather macabre if over-dressed figure, as a dark red stain began to spread out on his pillow.

TIMOTHY O'LEARY EMERGED from the small Fordham Law
School building on West 62nd Street, hoisted the backpack he
had just filled with the contents of his locker, and headed toward Columbus Avenue. Law school finished. The bar exam
behind him. A job offer accepted. It was 1968, and from now
on his life would take him elsewhere. He had taken this walk
to the subway countless times before, and this, it occurred to
him, might be his last time. He turned momentarily to look
back at the school, then moved on.

Yesterday morning, the call had come from Prescott B.
Steele, a partner in the Park Avenue law firm of Bradford,
Lord and Turner. Tim vaguely remembered Mr. Steele as another in the seemingly endless series of antiseptically clean,
coolly distant, but impressively erudite middle-aged lawyers
who had managed to make the prior autumn one of the most
uncomfortable in his life, as he trudged to interview after interview, from Wall Street to Park Avenue to Fifth Avenue, in
search of the elusive "going rate."

By the time Steele's call came, Tim's hopes of such a high-
toned start to his legal career had long since vanished. He had

eventually lowered his sights considerably, and finally worked out a decidedly less glamorous arrangement with Michael Finley, a solo general practitioner whose office was squeezed between an Italian restaurant and a check cashing service on Montague Street in Brooklyn. Mister Finley, who was apparently better known as Mickey Finn by his peers, focused on personal injury matters and other types of civil litigation, and occasionally represented criminal defendants. He had achieved some status on Court Street of late with a string of improbable successes in what had seemed to be hopeless slip and fall cases, and had decided that his elevated profile called for an expansion of his office. So, three months ago, Finley had sent postcards to a few of the local law schools to be pinned to their job placement bulletin boards. The cards informed the reader that an opportunity to learn the workings of the law at their most elemental and purest level was available to the recent graduate fortunate enough to be selected to "clerk" at the offices of Michael Moriarity Macauley Finley, Esq. In addition, an emolument of $2.50 per hour would be paid to this law clerk to assist him in defraying his personal expenses.

Nothing better having materialized and figuring that chasing ambulances was better than reading the New York Law Journal on the unemployment line, Tim had called Finley's office.

A woman, sounding old, answered. "Lawyer's office."

"Mr. Finley, please."

"Mr. Finley isn't in," she answered. "Who's calling?"

"This is Timothy O'Leary. I'm calling about the job opening for a law clerk."

"Wait a minute," she muttered suspiciously, like she might need to get the police on the other line.

A few seconds passed, and then a gruff male voice came on. Maybe she had indeed called the police.

"What school you from?"

"Fordham. Who is this?"

"Finley. Isn't that who you were calling?" It might as well

have been a cop.

"Oh. Mr. Finley. I'm sorry, I thought you weren't in. This is Timothy O'Leary. I—"

"I know who it is. I just don't want any of those Ivy League creeps around here. You start offering a chance like this, and good money to boot, and you never know who the hell's gonna show up. You want the job? Come down tomorrow at two and I'll take a look at you."

He hung up.

Tim had looked at the dead receiver in his hand for a full minute before he hung up himself, as if concerned that he might otherwise miss a gruff Finley afterthought.

The next day at Finley's office wasn't much better.

The office consisted of one large room, roughly partitioned by file boxes, coat racks and shelving into a waiting area, a secretarial area and the office of the honorable Michael Finley himself.

A woman of about 70 sat near a typewriter and a telephone, amidst an almost unbelievable pile of assorted papers that was presumably supported by a desk rather than being the peak of a paper mountain rising up from the office floor.

"Yes?" she said, looking at Tim warily.

"My name is Timothy O'Leary, from Fordham Law School. I have an appointment to see Mr. Finley about a job."

"Wait a minute," she said, as the telephone rang. "Lawyer's office," she advised the caller. Tim stole a peek at Mr. Finley in the back of the office. He appeared to be thinking, as opposed to writing or reading a book, or even sleeping, but it was difficult to be sure, due to the horizontal layers of cigar smoke that obscured his profile.

Just then, Tim's attention was diverted back to the lady amongst the pile of papers, as he heard her tell the caller that Mr. Finley was not in.

"No. He won't be in. He's trying a case in White Plains. Your matter will have to be adjourned. No. I'm sorry, there's an affidavit in the mail and we can't be responsible for the post office. You'll just have to call him next week for a new date. I have to get off now, the other phone is ringing."

She turned back to Tim. "Well, Mr. O'Leary, have a seat and I'll tell Mr. Finley you're here."

Continuing to stand, since the only available chair had its own stash of papers, Tim was becoming disoriented. He had heard this motherly figure tell a series of lies with such detachment that she could almost as easily have been one of Mr. Finley's most nefarious criminal clients. And now, although she had just said she would tell Mr. Finley he was here for his interview, she seemed instead to be burrowing around under the mountain of papers for something she had misplaced. The intensity with which she pursued this search, causing various papers to slide off the top of the pile and onto the floor, led Tim to momentarily consider the possibility that perhaps she was hunting for a card imprinted with a perfect act of contrition to which she might refer on the occasions of such dissembling.

This speculation ended when a loud buzzer sounded in the vicinity of Mr. Finley, and the elderly lady immediately thereafter ceased her efforts. Obviously, she had found and activated an intercom system of some sort. Finley at once looked up and began waving away the clouds of cigar smoke.

"O'Reilly? Is that you? Come back here, kid."

Tim figured this meant him, so he stepped between the paper mountain and an upright wooden coat rack, made his way past a short row of bookshelves and a five-drawer file cabinet, and came face to face with Michael Finley.

Finley was a man of some girth and seemed to be of short stature, although Tim could not be sure since Finley never rose to his feet. Instead, the lawyer remained seated with his feet propped on a scarred oak desk, as his fingers rotated a short thick cigar which protruded from the corner of his mouth. He squinted through the smoke at Tim.

"Sit down, O'Reilly. Let's get this started. I'm a busy man."

"It's O'Leary, Mr. Finley."

"O'Reilly? O'Leary? Whatever! Sit down."

Tim sat but remained silent, still perplexed.

"What kind of grades you getting?"

Tim, now on familiar ground, found his voice. "I have a B plus average, almost an A minus. I should graduate in the top ten percent of my class."

"Yeah? Well, don't get carried away with yourself. I used to get Cs myself at Brooklyn Law, but nobody asks about that once you get into a courtroom. Don't get me wrong, kid. I don't want any dummy working for me, but some of these Ivy League jackasses walk around with their diplomas on their sleeves. They act like you should kiss their wing-tip shoes and ask forgiveness for your weak mind and loose morals. And even when you beat them, they can't believe you were right. They figure you bought the judge or something, or that he was just as dumb as you, so they call it a Club-house Decision and appeal. Then what happens? Your client is tired, he's broke, he wants that money so bad he can taste it. So he makes you settle cheap, and those damn Ivies act as smug as one of your nuns when the bad girl at school gets pregnant. Just once, just once, O'Leary, I want to get a case against those bastards that I can carry all the way without them being able to bleed my client dry with their motions, and demands for documents, and every other damn harass-ment they can dream up with their big budgets and small minds."

Finley stopped, narrowed his eyelids, and began puffing furiously at his cigar. He was quite obviously in the midst of a subject which caused him great agitation, and his distant gaze made Tim wonder if Finley had forgotten that he was there.

"I certainly don't mean to imply that I haven't got a great deal to learn, Mr. Finley. I was just trying to answer your question."

Finley made no response, and seemed to be slipping back

within his envelope of cigar smoke. Abruptly, he began to speak again. "I had a closing last week. This other lawyer was from Harvard Law School—his degree was on the wall alongside the conference room table—you couldn't miss it. His client was selling an old house in Prospect Park South to my friend Joey Perroni. Joey figures the area's on its way back if they can just get the riffraff and the hippies out of there. So, this Harvard jerk, whose first name is Skip or Biff or something, drags the closing out for two and half hours because he says we have to follow an agenda. An agenda! He did everything but put a wax seal on the deed.

"And you know what? When he got to the end of his agenda, he got up, shook hands all around and started walking out of the room with his client. I stopped him. You know why?"

"Why?" Tim offered helpfully.

"To ask him if his client wanted any money for the building. The boob forgot the check! He must have been using the agenda for when one of his rich clients gave his building to charity."

Suddenly, Finley was on his feet, reaching for a hat on the radiator behind his chair. "I've gotta go. Seeing a client at Luger's at three. Nice meetin' ya, kid."

Tim stood as Finley rushed past and he realized for the first time that Finley was no more than five feet two or three. As Finley went by the front desk, he snapped to the secretary, "Clean this mess up, Mabel. We have clients coming in here, you know."

Opening the office door, he seemed to recall something and turned back momentarily. "You want the job, O'Reilly?"

Tim was stunned, but recovered quickly. He was beginning to adjust to Finley's rhythm.

"Sure," he said.

"When can you start?" retorted Finley.

"Right after the bar exam, Mr. Finley. In July."

"Okay. Call me then. If I'm still here, you've got a job.

Oh, and call me Mickey, Mickey Finn. That's what every-
body else does." Finley closed the door, caught his coat in it,
reopened the door to release himself, and was gone.

Three months later, having graduated, suffered through a
six-week cram course and then a two-day bar examination,
Tim was just about ready to call Finley to see about getting
started. Instead, the call came from Mr. Steele.

Tim was in many ways more comfortable with the Mickey Finns of this world than with Prescott B. Steele, but he
had to admit that there had been no real hesitation on his
part in accepting the new offer. For one thing, Bradford, Lord
and Turner paid the "going rate," which had just gone up
to $15,000 a year. That would go a lot further than $2.50
an hour, especially when there were nearly $10,000 in stu-
dent loans to repay. For another, it had occurred to him that
there wasn't even a chair for him at Finley's office, much less
a desk, and he wasn't quite ready to forsake *all* of the pre-
rogatives of his new profession. In any case, his decision was
quickly made, and communicated at once to Finley—there
was no point in having the prospect of that task cast a pall
over what he knew would be a pleasant period of growing
satisfaction about the offer just received.

Finley was understandably miffed, although more at
Tim's selection of an Ivy League-dominated firm than at the
loss of Tim himself. With respect to the latter, Finley had just
discovered a new internship program that had been initiated
at Brooklyn Law School to provide third-year law students
the opportunity, without pay, to learn the day-to-day aspects
of their chosen profession under the tutelage of practicing
attorneys. After all, he reasoned, $2.50 an hour can add up
very quickly, and he had so informed Mabel, reminding her
that her own more than generous $2.25 hourly rate was a
heavy burden for an honest lawyer trying to make a decent
living. In fact, he had told her, the amount might have to
be reviewed now that she was about to start receiving social security checks, largely as a result of his employment

tax payments over the 30 years she had been working at his office. Mabel was unimpressed by his logic, but had made no response, being distracted at the moment by a search she was conducting for the sandwich she had brought to the office for lunch. It had apparently been buried under some files Finley had dumped on her desk when he returned from court that morning. In any event, it would all be moot now and there would be no salary "adjustment." Finley picked up the phone and called his alma mater.

So, plans made, Tim left the law school that late July afternoon and walked to the subway to start his trip back to his father's home in Connecticut, where he planned to spend two weeks before embarking on his career.

3

TIM STEPPED OFF THE NEW HAVEN TRAIN in Bridgeport, Connecticut after the long ride from Grand Central Station, exhilarated by the late afternoon warmth, his new prospects and, as usual, a feeling of freedom after having escaped the confines of Manhattan. He looked forward to relaxing at his father's house before starting his job at Bradford, Lord and Turner. Intoxicated with his new sense of financial well-being, he decided to spring for a taxi rather than ask his father to pick him up. He soon was bumping along in the back seat of a beat up 1962 Chevy heading down Water Street toward the Connecticut Turnpike.

Tim's family's house had always been easy to find, especially for one traveling on the Turnpike. It was located immediately adjacent to and under an elevated portion of the road, and was clearly marked by a huge billboard rising up from the back yard.

The billboard had been a minor landmark in Tim's neighborhood since his childhood. It had been his father's idea of a way to turn the noxious proximity of the Turnpike into an income-producing asset and, fortunately for Tim, had been installed before he was old enough to be embarrassed by it. He only came to a realization of its uniqueness gradually and, mercifully, with but minor damage to his pride.

Tim did remember one time when the billboard caused a major family crisis, although less from the fact that it was there than from what was on it. When Tim was about nine years old, a period of several months passed without a paying message on the board. Increasingly concerned with this temporary dislocation in his cash flow, Tim's father consulted a local ad agency about the problem. For two weeks, Mr. O'Leary's agitation grew steadily, as the agency reported again and again that it was having no luck. Finally, however, the telephone rang late one afternoon with news of an opportunity.

"Yo," answered Mr. O'Leary.

His face brightened.

"Great, what is it?"

His face clouded over, as Tim watched with growing interest.

"What?" his father barked. He began to squint, as if to better focus on this new development.

"Now give me that again ... All of us? ... That much money? ... Yeah. I see ... Oh, what the hell. We'll do it. I'll bring the family down tomorrow morning."

The next day, Tim, his mother, looking somewhat strained, his father and his two sisters, all dressed in their best clothes, drove to a small photographer's studio in downtown Bridgeport and had their family picture taken. Several weeks later, as Tim left for school one morning, workmen on scaffolding were in his backyard preparing the billboard for a new message.

Tim brought his lunch to school, since both of his parents worked, but a number of the other children went home each day at lunchtime. That afternoon at school, he was twice victimized by "whoopie" cushions placed on his chair just before he sat down. Someone else flipped a stink bomb through a hedge onto the sidewalk in front of him on his way home. And a boy in a group of giggling children he passed a few blocks from his house called out to him as he went by, "Hey, Tim, I hear you're a real regular guy!"

As Tim turned the corner into his block, he began to understand the day's sequence of events. Above his house, on the billboard, was plastered the new poster—a gargantuan family portrait framed by the message, "I insist that my whole family use chocolate flavored Ex-Lax. Their flush of health is my reward!"

Realizing at last what had happened, Tim suddenly felt as if every pair of eyes in the neighborhood was on him, that he was at the moment the subject of every conversation (as his family may in fact have been), and that his life had suddenly, irrevocably, come to an end. He ran for his house, fearful of the consequences should anyone step out into the sidewalk and block his path, and fully intending, once he had entered the house, never to emerge.

Once inside, he was surprised to see that his mother was home. She looked like she was at a wake for someone close—brave but pained—sitting in a chair in a darkened living room, staring at the sunlight glowing around the edges of a drawn shade. Tim's sisters stood in front of her, eyes red, cheeks wet.

"Mom, you've got to make him take it down. You've got to," pleaded Katie.

"If he doesn't, I'm leaving," threatened Cissy.

"No one will ever call me again. I'll never have another date," declared Katie.

"You never had one before anyway," rejoined Cissy, unable to resist the temptation even in this time of crisis.

Katie turned on her sister, tears brimming, "Oh, no? What about Jimmy Nichols at the fair?"

"That wasn't a date. He just took you on a ride so he could grab at you in the scary parts. He didn't even walk you home," Cissy shot back.

Katie's lower lip began quivering uncontrollably and the tears streamed down her face. Unable to speak further, she grabbed her younger sister by the hair and started shaking her furiously. Cissy fought back as well as she could, with kicks, scratches and a few attempted bites.

Tim, seeing his sisters thus occupied, took the opportunity to approach his mother.

"Mom, our picture's on the billboard. You've got to do something," he said.

Mrs. O'Leary looked up at Tim, noticing for the first time that he was home. Then she looked over at the girls, who had just knocked over a chair but who were beginning to tire from their efforts.

"Katiencissy! Stop it! Stop it!" said Mrs. O'Leary, raising her voice just enough to be heard above the girls' screaming. Katie released her younger sister with some relief, since Cissy's wiry tenacity was beginning to overcome Katie's superiority in size and weight.

"Come into the kitchen, children. You, too, Timmy," said Mrs. O'Leary, as she gently nudged Tim between his angry sisters and steered all three into the kitchen. As she passed the darkened window which had captivated her attention moments earlier, she reached over and gave the shade a tug. Releasing it, her grave expression softened into one of determination as the room flooded with light.

Once in the kitchen, she sat the three children at the table and poured each of them a glass of milk. She took a Three Musketeers bar from the freezer, cut it into thirds and placed the sections in front of them. Then she returned to the living room, closing the door behind her.

Bits of her end of a telephone conversation could be heard through the door. Though the words themselves were indistinct, the tenor of their mother's voice was uncharacteristically firm, almost commanding, and the sound of the phone being returned to its cradle was sharp and final. Then there was silence.

After fifteen minutes, Tim peeked into the living room, where his mother was sitting placidly, gazing out the now unshaded window. He closed the door and walked softly back to the kitchen table, where he and his sisters continued to gripe about the events of the day, albeit with less passion than Katie and Cissy had displayed earlier.

An hour passed before they heard the doorbell ring. A few minutes later they heard sounds in the backyard, and, looking out through the kitchen window, they saw workmen raising ladders to the scaffolding that ran the length of the bottom of the billboard. Then, as they watched, the workmen ascended the ladders and set to work painting out the message on the billboard.

Each time a workman dipped a paint roller attached to a long pole into his large tray of whitewash, and then raised the roller to the offending message, Tim's spirits rose. He knew the teasing from his friends would not disappear as easily as the billboard's contents were now surrendering to the whitewash, but there was something vaguely pleasing about the way his mother's decisive action had changed the direction of the crisis and brought a moment of pride where only mortification had been before.

Life left Tim little time to dwell on this sensation, however, as the repercussions of his mother's action got underway even before the O'Leary family had completely vanished from the billboard.

"What the hell is going on here? What do you think you're doing to that billboard?"

The "billboard" sounded more like "Bill Bard." Tim knew that his father was home.

The workmen stopped their painting, poles and rollers poised, whitewash dripping on the scaffolding and the dirt below. They looked quizzically at Mrs. O'Leary, and then back to her husband, both of whom were also in the yard.

"Mah-gret, what's the meaning of this? What have yuh done?" he demanded, turning on her.

She fell apart, disintegrating before Tim's eyes. Her hands, which had been balled in fists resting on her narrow hips, were open now and extended toward her husband. The set of her jaw had slackened and she spoke words of supplication, not command.

"Tim, the kids were so upset, everyone teasing them and all, and all the neighbors were talking. I was ashamed to go out today. Please don't let them put it up again. Please ..." Then she broke down completely and ran into the house. Tim heard the door slam and his mother's footsteps pounding up the stairs as she fled his father's wrath.

He turned back to the kitchen window to see his father order the men down off the scaffolding, argue with them briefly over their right to compensation for this act of desecration and then hand one of them some bills as the other packed to leave. The billboard's message had been completely obliterated, although his father's face was still visible in a clear space in a sea of whitewash.

For several days afterward, an air of tension pervaded the O'Leary house. Representatives of the laxative company visited on several occasions, discussing with Tim's father the mechanics of raising the sign again. Eventually, however, a complication appeared to arise, and, after a few more heated discussions, the men left and were not heard from again.

When Tim asked his father about it one day, he was told that there was a problem with the papers that had been signed, and that the matter was now "in the hands of the lawyers," the last word coming out like "liars," and confusing Tim even more. What he eventually learned was that his father had signed his mother's name to the consent forms for the use of the family picture, and that this had come to light only after the whitewash incident. Actually, if he had asked her to sign in the first place, she certainly would have, but after that day she would not be a party to any such agreement. Although she never again summoned the nerve to lead an outright rebellion, she clung to this one victory and stubbornly refused to sign a paper which would completely erase her moment of triumph.

Tim, once he had learned both the proper pronunciation and the meaning of the word "lawyers," would in later years remember this experience as one of the most significant in his life. For one thing, he had seen the impact of a decisive act, even when the actor was otherwise weak. And for another, he had seen for the first time the pervasive influence of an as yet unmet phenomenon—the lawyer.

4

AS TIM'S TAXICAB PULLED UP in front of the Bridgeport house, he raised his eyes to the billboard. The current message had to do with air travel, presumably not something which would have ever been a subject of controversy in the O'Leary home. Tim got out of the cab, paid the driver and walked up the short path to his front door. He rang the bell, and a few seconds later his father opened the door.

"Timmy Boy! I'm glad to see you. Come in. How was the bar exam?"

"Hi Pop. It was hard but it's over."

"Well, good. Sit down in the living room and we'll have a drink to celebrate the start of your vacation."

Tim went in and sat on the couch, while his father poured two beers and two shot glasses of Four Roses whiskey. The older man set a beer and a shot on the coffee table in front of his son, did the same for himself on the table next to his armchair and then sat down facing Tim.

"So, how is Mickey Finn?"

"I'm not going to work for Mr. Finley, Pop. I took another job."

"In Brooklyn?"

"No, in Manhattan. On Park Avenue. With a big old line law firm."

"No kidding? A big shot, huh? But why on Park? Why not go all the way—Wall Street?"

"Some of the old firms are uptown now. Mine was downtown for years, until it took new offices on Park Avenue last year."

His father seemed disappointed to hear this. Maybe he figured it was a shame that, after trying so hard to get somewhere, his son had found upon arriving that the occupants had moved. As if in sympathy, he reached over to pick up his shot glass, emptied its contents into the beer, and took a healthy swallow of the "boilermaker."

Tim sipped his beer, ignoring the whiskey which had been poured for him.

"How are Katie and Cissy?" he asked.

"Fine!" his father replied. "Katie was over last weekend with her two kids. Her doctor husband was doing rounds at Bridgeport Hospital, so he couldn't make it."

"He doesn't get over here often, does he?"

"No, I guess medicine keeps a man pretty busy. A woman, too—Cissy's working double shifts this week. One more year in the classroom and she gets her nursing degree."

The older man paused to finish his drink. Then, his voice a bit thick, said "You've all done fine. It's only too bad your mother, rest her soul, couldn't have lived to see it."

"I'm sure she can see it, Pop, from where she is now. And I'm sure she's proud of you, too, for seeing us all through," Tim said sympathetically. And then, a twinkle in his eye, he added, "Even if you did need the help of the billboard at times to make ends meet."

His father brightened immediately. "Ah, the billboard. Smartest move I ever made. Your mother as much as admitted that to me on more than one occasion, even if she did act a bit peevish about one sign we had up there for awhile. You probably don't remember that."

"Oh, I remember it well," said Tim, "It was—"

"Talking about remembering," interrupted his father, "I almost forgot. I was at Smokey's last night and I ran into someone you used to know. We were talking about you."

"Who was that?"

"Marge Conley. Remember her?"

"Sure. She went to grade school with me. She was thin and sort of pretty—and very smart. What's she up to now?"

"She's a private eye. Works out of New Haven."

"A private eye? You mean an investigator, a private detective? How could a girl do that?"

"She said the guidance counselor at her high school tried to push her and the other smart girls who wanted to go to college into teaching or social work, or even Gibbs for secretarial. Her friends told her she should just get married and start a family. She said the seniors in her class had a motto, 'A ring by spring.' She wanted no part of that, so she decided to try something different. If you ask me, Marge is a little wacky. But she's fun. She insisted on buying me a beer in Smokey's, and we talked over old times. You ought to look her up. Lawyers need to know private eyes to help them with their cases."

"Not 'Wall Street' lawyers, Pop."

"Well, look her up anyway. I promised I'd have you call her when you came home. She'd like to see you."

"Okay." Tim stood up and stretched. "I'm going upstairs for a nap. When I get up, I'll treat you to dinner at Smokey's."

"Not tonight, Tim. I'm due at the K of C at seven, and we'll be eating over there. Maybe tomorrow."

"Okay. See you later." As Tim turned around and headed for the stairs, he noticed his father pick up Tim's full shot glass and carry it to the piano, which was covered with family photographs. He lifted the glass toward the picture of Tim's late mother which hung over the piano, smiled, and drained off its contents.

Tim smiled, winked at the photograph, and went up to bed.

When he woke up, it was half light. Disoriented for a moment, Tim wondered whether it was evening or early morning. Checking his new calendar watch and realizing the date had not changed, he decided he had not slept through the night, but the messages his stomach was sending up told him he was as hungry as if he had. He rolled out of bed and stumbled from the darkening bedroom toward the stairway to head downstairs.

Flipping on the overhead light as he entered the kitchen, Tim headed straight for the refrigerator. He peered inside, looking for something to eat. Instead, however, he found eight cans of Schaefer beer, three eggs, a container of orange juice, a pint of milk, some coffee and four cigars. Now he knew why his father was having his dinner at the Knights of Columbus.

He grabbed one of the beers, slammed the refrigerator door shut, and sat down at the kitchen table to contemplate his situation. As he worked on the beer and looked out the kitchen window at the darkening sky, the overhead lights came on to illuminate the billboard, and he noticed its message for the second time that day. It featured a pretty blonde on a white sand beach on some tropical isle, where she had apparently been deposited by the airline in question, ostensibly without the normal inconveniences of long check-in lines, flight delays, passport controls and suspicious customs officers, tedious and uncomfortable airport-to-hotel transfers, and the rest of the exhausting and frustrating business of flying to paradise. Nevertheless, Tim found the picture appealing. After three months of forced asceticism, and studying first for third-year final exams and then for the bar exam, getting little sleep and less recreation, he was the perfect subject for the airline's invitation. The idea of being on that beach was just what the doctor ordered, and he was sure that the doctor would also insist that he be there with that woman.

Or maybe with any woman.

And then he remembered. He had promised his father he would call Marge Conley. His image of her would never be confused with the girl on the billboard. She wasn't even blonde. But he was in Bridgeport, after all, and he had to be realistic. He picked up the phone book.

An hour later he was sitting at one of the back tables at Smokey's Bar and Grill with Marge Conley. She had insisted that they meet there despite his suggestion that he take her to dinner at one of the fancier restaurants down by the water. Secretly, he was glad at her insistence. There was never a wait for a table at Smokey's. The atmosphere and attire were casual at best, and the food was ample and satisfying, if a bit greasy and unhealthy. The bar dominated one side of the room with its solid, albeit inelegant, presence. The wall behind it was paneled with mirrors, reflecting back the rows of liquor bottles stacked before it and, beyond them, the bar itself and the murkier recesses of the room.

Not that the room was particularly large. It was just that, at a time when people were starting to worry about smoking, almost every patron of Smokey's held fast to his or her habit. By late evening visibility was diminishing rapidly as their puffing increased in intensity.

Marge Conley took a drag on her own cigarette and, exhaling with her lower lip jutting out slightly so that the smoke was directed upwards, away from his face, looked at him reflectively. She was still thin, but now in her mid-twenties she had filled out in places that gave her an appearance of softness and sensuality. Her short reddish-brown hair seemed to leap off her head in every imaginable direction, curls competing with waves, and waves with straight lines. The look could have been the product of some mad, but brilliant, stylist who had forgotten how long it would take a girl with a comb and brush to reproduce this creation on a daily basis. For the time being, however, order prevailed, and the effect was pleasing. Marge's green eyes, dark eyebrows, slender nose and full lips

were well-framed by her storm-tossed sea of a coiffure. Tim
was impressed. He had expected her to look like a tall fourth
grader.

Tim suddenly realized he was about to cough, but held
off just long enough to ask Marge if she had ever thought of
giving up smoking.

"Every day, Tim. I'm down to half a pack a day, and I
plan to go cold turkey when Lent rolls around."

"You think that'll work?"

"Sure. It worked the last three years."

"But you're still smoking."

"Well, I went back. This time maybe I can make it permanent. Hey, enough about that. I hear you got a job down in
Brooklyn—with one of those Court Street lawyers."

"I did," said Tim, "but I'm not taking it. I just got a job
with one of the big Wall Street firms. Well, not really Wall
Street—they moved up to Park Avenue last year—but you
know what I mean. I'm going to take that instead."

"Good for you," said Marge, seeming genuinely pleased
for him. "Was your father happy? When I saw him yesterday,
he didn't seem to know about it."

"Oh, he was happy, all right, but I think he was a little
confused about the news that 'Wall Street lawyers' work on
Park Avenue and Fifth Avenue now."

"Oh, he'll get used to it," said Marge. "Actually, though,
I know an awful lot of the people from Yale wind up at the
big old line firms, but I haven't heard of too many Fordham boys sneaking in. We may have to set you up in a crash
course at one of the local finishing schools to get you ready."

Tim laughed, but he knew very well what she meant. His
background was not the type most highly sought after at
firms like Bradford, Lord and Turner. It was one of the last
bastions of old money attorneys with a client roster packed
with blue blood social register types. He knew he might be
out of his element there. Nevertheless, a salary of $15,000,
for someone who did not even know yet whether he had

passed the bar exam, could assuage a multitude of potential slights.

"So, Tim," said Marge. "Since you're about to become a big shot, why don't you start acting like one and buy a poor working girl another drink and some dinner?"

"Sure," said Tim, embarrassed. He lurched forward from the bench and peered through the gloom, trying to catch a glimpse of the one waitress employed by Smokey's Bar and Grill. As he did so, he hit his head on the low-hanging Tiffany lamp that illuminated their table, sending it swinging in a wild arc, and getting him the attention not only of the waitress but also of the other seven patrons of Smokey's, all of whom were sitting at the bar.

"Hey, Marge!" crowed one old hen, showing her few remaining teeth in a grin that crinkled her purplish face into a thousand parts. "Take it easy on that guy. Wad'ja do? Show'm some pitchers ya took of'm over 't th' motel? Serves 'm right fer givin' his wife enough money so's she could hire a smart private eye like you." She and the others at the bar broke up in boozy hysterics.

Marge laughed, too, and yelled back, "Mind your own business, Blossom, or I'll show Harry some of the shots I got of you over at the motel last week."

"Blossom" let out a howl, and smacked a wizened little codger sitting next to her on the back. The blow caused him to spray a mouthful of unswallowed beer right toward the bartender, who managed to avoid the worst of it by nimbly jumping back out of range.

"For Chris' sake, Harry!" the bartender yelled. "Would you watch what you're doing?"

Harry, apparently unable to hear or comprehend much of this, at first looked startled and frightened by the bartender's menacing countenance. When he saw Blossom's grin, though, he seemed to figure out there was something funny going on. He burst out in a cackling laugh, then started slapping the other patrons on the back as well. The bar again dissolved in a burst of mirthfulness.

Marge, still laughing, turned back to Tim, who looked devastated. Seeing his expression, her face softened, and she leaned over and put her hand on his arm. As she did so, the top of her blouse parted and he could see the gentle swelling of her breasts as they disappeared into the lacy top of her under things. The warmth of her touch, the soft femininity of her face and body, and the gentleness of her gesture infatuated and confused him, so at variance was it with the raucous conviviality she had shown toward her cronies at the bar just a moment before. He resolved to get to know her better.

5

DURING TIM'S TWO-WEEK VACATION, he and Marge had dinner together almost every night. They always went to Smokey's, where they were both comfortable. The bar regulars grew used to seeing Tim with Marge, and gradually accepted him as her friend, giving him the nickname "Heads." Tim eventually learned that it was his run-in with the Tiffany lamp that had earned him the moniker. Shirley, the waitress, whom they all addressed as "Toots," became familiar with their practice of having a few drinks before they ate. She left them alone, except to replenish their drinks, while they talked.

And talk they did. For hours at times, at the end of the day, after Marge had closed her office and driven over from New Haven, about 20 miles away. Tim would come in from whatever he was doing, say hello to the regulars and head for the booth at the back where he and Marge usually sat. He would endure the obligatory shouts like, "Watch out for the lamp, Heads. Let Toots hold it out of the way for you so you can sit down. Hey Toots, c'mere and help Heads, willya?" and so on. He knew they would lose interest in a minute or two and be drawn back to the black and white television set over the bar, or to their own conversation. Anyway, he realized, he enjoyed the good cheer and warmth of the place, and was glad to be a part of it.

Once they had settled in each evening, and Toots had brought them their drinks—a Scotch and water for Marge and a beer for Tim—they would fall into the easy conversational pattern of old friends. At first, they brought themselves up to date on the dozen or more years that had passed since they remembered seeing one another last.

She had attended Bridgeport High after they graduated from grade school, played on the girl's basketball team and run middle distance for the track team during her first few years there. Marge found, however, that she simply was neither agile enough nor fast enough to keep pace with the more talented girls on those teams. She needed to do well enough academically to win a scholarship to college, which her parents could not otherwise afford, so she dropped sports and concentrated on her studies. The results had been even better than she'd anticipated. She graduated first in her class and won a four year scholarship to Yale, where she majored in political science and journalism, and made a good enough impression to earn a position on the prestigious Yale Daily News, informally referred to as the "Yalie Daily." As she approached graduation, though, she concluded that she was most interested in pursuing something exciting like law enforcement or investigative work. At the same time, she began to realize that Betty Friedan's *The Feminine Mystique* and her newly-founded National Organization for Women had generated more irritation than job openings in these male-dominated fields. While women were now tolerated in some of the professions and the lower levels of the business world, it was still considered to be inappropriate for them to enter fields such as hard core police work, where they were hired reluctantly if ever, and never really accepted by their peers. Even if she had been able to land a job in the police department, the idea of working within a male-dominated bureaucracy was too restrictive for her independent spirit. A few women were now studying law, but she had no interest in being some firm's token female attorney whiling away her time in their law library. So she passed on law school, earned an advanced degree in criminology, and then, just over one year ago, opened her own private investigation agency in New Haven.

From what she told Tim, it had not been an easy year, as she attempted to break into a profession dominated by retired male police officers. Her license had been held up, until calls by her uncle to a few of his well-placed friends in the State Human Rights Commission seemed to break up the logjam. She had struggled to find business, and at times questioned her decision to eschew the public payroll for what she had naively expected would be an exciting and fulfilling career from day one. She had dreamed of uncovering information and solving mysteries, with appropriate payment for her efforts as well as the gratitude of those who had sought her out in their times of trouble. Compared to her unbroken string of academic successes, starting a business and struggling to obtain clients was a humbling experience, making her realize that life outside the classroom might prove to be a lot harder than life within, but she had persevered. The few clients who had not beaten a hasty retreat from her office after realizing that the Conley of Conley Investigations was a woman had generally been more than satisfied with the results, and were beginning to spread the word about her competence. It was starting to look like she was going to make it, and she was delighted.

Tim's story was hardly past the stage of emerging from the academic cocoon, but it had also reached a point of positive expectations. He and Marge had parted company after the eighth grade. He had attended the local Catholic high school and then Fairfield University, living at home all the while, since his father could manage the tuition but not the room and board, and Tim's grades, while good, were not of scholarship caliber. Following his graduation from Fairfield, he went down to New York City to attend the Fordham University School of Law.

Fordham University had traditionally been associated with The Bronx, where its Rose Hill campus was located, but the law school had always operated in Manhattan, most recently in a building on West 62nd Street across from the new Lincoln Center, which was being developed as part of an effort to revive an area of West Side Manhattan that had seen better days. Tim spent the next three years there, commuting by subway to an uncle's home in Queens until eventually sharing a small fourth floor walkup apartment near the law school with a classmate. Tim worked in the law school's library on weekdays, and at an area restaurant on weekends, to cover expenses. He studied and worked almost all of the time, made some new friends in between and partied with them when he could. Somewhere along the way he had finished growing up, it seemed, and he surprised himself when he realized that he had actually become an exceptional student. When he graduated, he knew he would never be a kid again, but wasn't too sure yet that he would make a good adult.

As Tim and Marge talked, about their pasts and their futures, and about anything else that came to mind, and kibitzed with Blossom and Harry and Toots and the other bar regulars, a closeness began to develop. Both of them noticed only gradually, not objecting to it, but not rushing the process, either. Their feelings started manifesting themselves in small ways—her hand resting on his arm while they talked, or his fingers gently kneading the back of her neck after she had suffered a particularly rough day, and a little tickling and playful pushing here and there when one of them acted too somber or pompous.

One night toward the end of the second week, Tim and Marge decided to pay a call on Tim's father. The subject of his billboard had come up in their conversation and Marge confessed that she had never actually seen it.

When they arrived at the house, the lights were off. A note on the kitchen table from Tim's father said he had been invited on a weekend fishing trip out on Cape Cod. He and his cronies had left late that afternoon, and he would not return until Sunday. He promised to bring back some striped bass for Tim.

"Striped bass," laughed Tim. "I hope so. Last time he came back with about a hundred pounds of mackerel and a couple dozen sea robins. He gave them to everyone on the block, but most of our neighbors didn't like mackerel very much, and no one likes sea robins. So they smiled, thanked him, closed their front doors and went right out the back to dump the fish in the garbage. It was a holiday weekend, and the garbage men didn't pick up for about five days. By that time, the neighborhood smelled so bad that some of the people on the next block complained to the Board of Health."

"I guess I had better steer clear of your father next week," said Marge. "I can do without any mackerel or whatever you called those other things."

"Let's sit, Marge," said Tim, pointing to the living room couch. "We might as well stay for a while. Can I get you a beer? My father doesn't keep any Scotch."

"Sure, Tim. That will be fine."

Tim poured two beers and brought them in to the living room. He put them on the coffee table in front of the couch and then sat down next to Marge.

"So, I never asked you. How was the work week?"

"Good, Tim," she said softly, "Both of these weeks have been good. The work has been coming along, but I've enjoyed the evenings with you the best."

"It's been nice for me, too. Very nice. I'm going to miss you next week."

They were silent for a moment, and then Tim leaned over and took the glass from Marge's hand. He placed both his and hers on the coffee table, and turned back to her.

She was waiting for him.

They kissed, and he was surprised at how full and soft her lips were. He put his right arm around her shoulders, and she rested the back of her head against it, as they continued to kiss one another softly and tenderly for several minutes. And then she began to touch his face and hair with her hand, as her lips slowly parted.

Tim reached for Marge with his left hand, encircling her now as he caressed her thigh, her hip, and then, as she took his hand in hers and raised it to herself, her breasts.

He fondled her hungrily but tenderly, his excitement increasing as he felt her nipples harden and press against his hand through her blouse. She murmured encouragement, and he unbuttoned the blouse, reaching inside and sliding his hand under her bra until he cupped one of her soft breasts and massaged it slowly. Removing it from the bra, he lifted her breast gently and lowered his head to her and now marveled in turn at her softness and fullness as his lips touched there.

Marge shifted and with her right hand undid the top buttons of his shirt. Reaching behind him she slid her cold hand under his collar and over his back, drawing him to her as she lowered herself on the couch. Tim, gratefully, settled in next to her and continuing to kiss her breasts, moved his hand under her skirt.

When his hand reached her panties, he found them moist and, panting now, he moved his fingers beneath them and into her. Moaning, she pulled him closer, digging her fingernails into his back as she did so.

"Heads," she whispered, "take your clothes off. We've got work to do."

6

WHEN TIM EMERGED from Grand Central Station the following Monday morning, having commuted from Bridgeport for his first day of work as a neophyte lawyer, he could already feel droplets of sweat beginning to form under his collar and roll down his back. He knew Manhattan's cauldron-like August weather would wilt his starched shirt and brand new wool suit in a matter of minutes. He began to fantasize a horrified Prescott B. Steele, upon seeing this creature dripping with sweat and looking like a homeless street person wearing an unpressed suit freshly loaned to him by the Salvation Army, immediately regretting his decision to extend an offer of employment to such an unlikely prospect. It went something like this:

"Oh, why it's you, Mr. O'Leary." Steele's face at first reddens, and then quickly registers outright revulsion as Tim, rising from the chair in the waiting room, leaves a visibly moist silhouette imprinted on the chair's rich Moroccan leather. Tim reaches forward with his hand to shake Steele's, which is extended toward him, although somewhat tentatively. Leaning now, as Steele seems to shrink back slightly, perhaps recoiling from the smell of damp wool, Tim feels the moisture under his hair gather, then rush forward. Like flash floods, small rivulets of sweat gather at his hairline, tumble forward down his forehead and then spill over the tip of his nose— stopping only when they splash on Steele's hand, which Tim has somehow managed to grasp and hold only a few inches under his own nose.

"Ah. Well. Yes, young man. I—" Steele pulls his hand free so quickly that Tim, leaning much too far forward now, loses his balance and stumbles, instinctively grabbing for the nearest handhold—Prescott B. Steele's trousers—to support himself. The results are predictable.

Tim's reverie was suddenly interrupted by a slender fellow with a shaven head and outfitted in a saffron robe, who stepped in front of him as he approached 48th Street. Interspersing chants of "Hare Krishna" with attempts to sell him a vegetarian cookbook, the earnest missionary smiled and pressed a flower into Tim's hand. Refusing the proffered volume as politely as possible in his agitated state, Tim brushed by the smiling monk and kept walking north on Park Avenue.

299 Park Avenue was a modern 42-story office tower, gleaming now in the morning sunshine, but more intimidating than inviting to Tim as he entered the lobby with its marble walls and 20-foot ceilings. Tim edged his way into the crush of people rushing through the lobby toward the rows of elevators, there to be consumed by the mahogany-paneled boxes and shot upward to the building's life cells, its offices. They would nourish it for another day, bringing it to life as the thriving, throbbing, thrusting embodiment of the perfect financial machine that is New York City. Even while rechecking Bradford, Lord and Turner's floor location on the building directory, Tim began to feel himself drawn by the building's vitality.

"Damn!" he whispered to himself, joining the stream. "This sure beats Montague Street."

On the 33rd floor, he exited the elevator and, for the first time a part of it, entered the world of Bradford, Lord and Turner. In front of him were glass doors, and over them the firm's name, etched in brass. Through the doors he could see the firm's reception area and, beyond that, also with glass doors, a series of large rooms, including a library and a conference room. These, in turn, looked out through floor-to-ceiling windows over the spiky towers of East Side Manhattan and beyond to the East River and Queens.

Tim approached the receptionist who, unlike her counterpart at the office of Mickey Finn, had nary a scrap of paper on her polished desk. Her angelic face reminded him not so much of the model types that occupied many reception desks on the East Side, but instead of the more refined, and mature, beauty of Princess Grace of Monaco, whose storybook wedding to Prince Rainier of Monaco had enthralled Americans not so many years before. And when the receptionist welcomed him with her smile, he melted, although in a more pleasant way than he had earlier that morning on his walk from the train station.

"Good morning," she said softly, almost whispering. "Can I help you?" The scent of lilacs drifted toward Tim as he stood before her desk.

"Yes. My name is Tim O'Leary. I told Mr. Steele that I would be starting work today."

"Oh, Mr. O'Leary! It certainly is a pleasure to see you. Welcome to Bradford, Lord and Turner."

"Thank you," responded Tim appreciatively, smitten by the recognition as much as by her looks.

"My name is Eloise Jones. Mr. Steele is on vacation until Labor Day, but he left word that you would be arriving this morning. If you would take a seat, I will call one of the messengers to show you to your office."

Within minutes, he had been fetched from the reception area and shown to a decidedly less stunning section of the firm's offices where, he was told, he would be sharing space with another young attorney. His office mate was, however, away on vacation, so Tim had the office to himself for now.

The room was small, about twelve by fifteen feet, and it contained two oak desks, each with one chair for the occupant and another for a guest. The messenger, a soft-spoken young man in a dusty green blazer and scuffed shoes, pointed to the desk closer to the door and indicated to Tim that it was his. Tim, docile in the presence of an experienced hand, however low on the totem pole, sat down and began to thumb through an office procedure manual which had been left on his desk.

An hour later, he was still reading memos about vacations, sick days, charging copies to clients' accounts and other exciting topics when his telephone buzzed. He picked it up.

"Tim," said a male voice on the other end of the line, "This is Rem Watson. Welcome to the firm."

"Thank you," Tim replied, trying to remember who the caller was. "I'm happy to be here."

"Well, great. We're delighted to have you. Say, Tim, if you can spare me a few minutes, could you stop down at my office?"

"Sure, Mr. Watson. Be right down."

"Great Tim. But call me Rem. I'm on your floor—northeast corner."

"Be right there, Mr. Watson. Rem."

Tim almost fell off his chair in his haste to accept the invitation, all the while wondering what this Mr. Watson could think he might be doing that he could not break away from. He picked up two pencils and a pad of lined yellow paper that he found on his desk and hurried down the hall, trying to remember which way was north and which east.

The office of Remington Pratt Watson was immense—perhaps 20 feet square—and beautifully decorated with antiques and colonial reproductions. Sheer drapes filtered the strong sunshine entering the room from two adjoining exterior walls that were composed almost entirely of tinted glass. A few original oil paintings added interest to the interior walls, while a monstrous Kerman Persian rug covered most of the floor.

"Rem" Watson rose as Tim entered the office. He was the quintessential White Anglo Saxon Protestant, that curious breed of northern European Protestant which had dominated the commercial life of America for so many years up until, if not the present day, at least a generation or two ago. He was in his early middle age, probably about 50, tall and ruggedly trim and handsome. He gripped Tim's hand firmly and guided him to one of the French provincial, lightly-upholstered chairs on the visitors' side of his desk.

"Tim, it's great to have you with us. Ready for some work?"

"Sure, Mr. ... Rem. I hope I can help," said Tim, at the same time wondering what he could possibly know at this stage in his career that could be of any help to this urbane legal giant.

"Well, Tim, let me give you some of the background. Our client, Rex Simpson, died last week in a rather bizarre accident. I got a call from his office this morning. They said his maid had just found him, after letting herself into his apartment to do the Monday morning cleaning. Sounds like poor Rex had been dead for days. Fell and hit his head on a table. Then he must have dragged himself to his bed, where he just laid down and bled to death."

Watson stood and turned toward the windows. In the silence that followed, Tim, who had been furiously scribbling notes on the yellow pad while occasionally murmuring a sympathetic word, stopped for a moment and looked up.

"Why was he dead so long before they found him?" Tim asked. "Was he living alone?"

Watson turned back from the window. "Yes, he was. He and his wife had been estranged for quite awhile. Actually, they had just made it official with a divorce, but he lived alone in his Manhattan apartment for several years before that. I don't know where he got this maid, but I understand she was there only on Mondays. Other than that, no one would have been in the apartment on a regular basis."

Watson walked back to his chair and sat down. "Anyway, they will be wanting the firm to handle the estate, and I would like you to give us some help with that, since all of our estate lawyers seem to be tied up defending our clients' millions from the depredations of the Internal Revenue Service. It would be a big help if you could get things started by handling the probate proceeding. I know you're new, but it should be simple enough."

7

BACK IN HIS OFFICE, Tim sat down and opened the file given to him by Rem Watson. It was surprisingly small, containing several thin folders marked "Correspondence," "Assets," "Wills" and "Notes & Miscellaneous." The outside of the file was marked "Reginald V. Simpson, Esq. File No. 1027.3 (transfer from File No. 1027.2—Reginald V. and Mary Graham Simpson)."

Tim removed the correspondence folder from the file and opened it on the desk in front of him. It contained only two items—one being a carbon copy of a letter dated about a month prior, addressed to Simpson by Rem Watson. It read:

"Dear Rex:

I am enclosing a copy of your new Will, which you signed in the office yesterday. As we discussed, the original of the Will is being placed in our office Will safe, which is maintained under the supervision of Alice Tedesco, the office file manager. It is of course available to you should you need it for any purpose, but I would not recommend your removing it from the firm's custody, as there are serious consequences which may arise if a Will cannot be found after a client's death where it is shown to have been last in the client's possession.

Your prior Will is enclosed, as you requested, so that you can destroy it. Now that your divorce has become final, its provisions favoring your former spouse would have been revoked by operation of law in any event, but it is certainly your prerogative to destroy it if you wish to do so.

I enjoyed working with you, as always. Give me a ring for lunch someday soon.

Sincerely,

Rem"

The other item was also a copy of a letter from Rem Watson, dated a few weeks before the first, which read:

"Dear Rex:

As you requested, Austin Chamberlain has drawn a new Will for you, and a copy is enclosed for your review. The provisions of the Will are straightforward. The entire estate is left to your cousin Theodore Bracken, with no provision whatsoever being made for your brother Harold or his family. I regret, as you do, your estrangement from Harold, but I can assure you that the necessary precautions will be taken to prevent a successful contest of the Will by Harold should the occasion ever arise.

Please give me a call after you have had an opportunity to review the draft. We can then schedule an appointment for you to come into the office to execute the Will if it meets with your approval.

Sincerely,

Rem"

Intrigued by the possibility of lurking family bitterness in Mr. Simpson's life, which had apparently also been scarred recently by divorce, Tim returned the correspondence folder to the file and removed the folder marked "Notes & Miscellaneous." Opening the folder, its scribbled contents in sharp contrast to the neatly-typed letters in the correspondence file, Tim read Rem's mini-biography of Rex Simpson.

Rex, it appeared, was a man of notable professional

achievement but little luck in his personal life. He was a partner in a major New York law firm, past president of the Association of the Bar of the City of New York, and an occasional speaker at seminars for other securities law professionals. He'd served on the board of directors of numerous national corporations and charities, and was an advisor to Governor Rockefeller on fiscal issues relating to the New York securities markets. Although never having held prior judicial office, he was an oft-mentioned frontrunner for appointment as Judge of the United States Court of Appeals for the Second Circuit when a vacancy, which was expected at the end of the year, materialized. In short, he was a legal superstar.

His personal life was another story. He had tried marriage twice, both times unsuccessfully, with neither union producing an heir. His parents, the late Judge Clayton Simpson and Laura Dahlgren Simpson, were deceased. He had only one sibling, his brother Harold Simpson, from whom he had not heard in more than four years. The end of their already tenuous relationship had come when Rex informed his brother that he would no longer honor his repeated requests for funds and other assistance required from time to time to extricate him from various predicaments. There was some indication that Harold might have a family, albeit not the legitimate kind, but there was no confirmation of this in the file.

The only relative with whom Rex had developed a relationship was a first cousin (the file said "once removed") by the name of Theodore Bracken. This fellow, not much older than Tim, was a working man who lived on Long Island. Teddy, as Rex apparently called him, was a carpenter and had not yet married. Although sketchy, Rem's notes indicated that Rex was able to "let his hair down" with his cousin when visiting with him on Long Island to fish, reminisce about their shared recollections of their families, and otherwise enjoy a relationship without pretensions. Rex would also take his cousin on fishing and hunting trips in Canada and the Northwestern United States, or on weekend excursions to the Catskills and Adirondacks of upstate New York.

The notes concluded by briefly summarizing a meeting between Rex and Watson in June. In view of his recent divorce, Simpson had instructed Watson to draw up a new Will for him. It would leave his entire estate to his cousin and "good buddy," Teddy Bracken, completely disinheriting his estranged brother. No alternate beneficiary would be named, at least for the time being. Tim's inspection of the Will folder confirmed that this change of plan had in fact been effected in the new Will.

Just as Tim was about to extract the final folder from the file so that he could review Mr. Simpson's assets, a long, pointy nose was thrust through the door to his office ... followed by large ears ... and an Adam's apple. What confronted Tim was a tall stalk of a person from which these and various other sharp features protruded. Smiling gawkishly, the outlandish stick figure thrust his hand toward Tim, snapping his erector set physique straight as he did so. "Hi, pal," he said. "I'm Mike Green. How about some lunch?"

"Sure, great ... I mean, I'm Tim O'Leary and I ... do you work here?"

"What else?" laughed the happy stork. "They wouldn't pay me otherwise. I do litigation, which is where they stick all the nuts. C'mon, let's get something to eat and you can tell me what they have you doing so far."

8

TIM AND MIKE TOOK THE ELEVATOR down to the building lobby and walked out onto the now bustling sidewalk. With Mike leading the way, they dodged and twisted down Park Avenue, trying to avoid the hordes of office workers, tourists, and unidentifiable others, all equally anxious to get where they were going and back during the tantalizingly long but hopelessly short lunch hour. Tim marveled at Mike's adaptability to these conditions. He seemed to expand and contract to fit through the ever-changing passageways in this flooding herd, moving his limbs this way and that as if to simulate the fluctuating angles and shapes of an image viewed through a toy kaleidoscope.

They turned a corner into a small side street, Tim struggling to keep up with his new friend. "What do you think so far?" Green yelled back over his shoulder.

"Great! I can't believe how you maneuver through all these people. Where are we heading?"

"No! I mean how do you like BLT so far?"

"BLT?"

"Bradford, Lord and Turner. That's what some of us

working stiffs call it, at least when the upper classes aren't around."

"Oh, the office. That's great too. I haven't really met anyone, but I'm working on a case already."

Having lost some of his concentration on this urban version of white water rafting, Tim walked right into the back of a man who was rummaging through a trash receptacle near the curb. The resulting collision between the vagrant and the trash can caused a sufficient commotion to momentarily halt the headlong flow of humanity along the sidewalk. After his initial shocked yelp, the man turned and realized what had happened, and immediately began lacing into Tim with a stream of invective.

Although most of the pedestrians surged forward after their initial pause, a few arrested their progress and idled in the vicinity, waiting to see what might develop. Tim, reddening more deeply with every passing second, desperately scanned the sidewalk for an escape route. The crowd continued to build, drawn more by the interest of the few who had first stopped than by the spectacle itself. Tim finally began to stammer an apology to his victim-turned-attacker, who hardly paused long enough to hear it before resuming his "Who do you people think you are?" assault. Just then, however, someone pushed past the aggrieved victim, grabbed Tim's arm and pulled him roughly away from the scene. Tim turned and saw that it was Mike Green, who was now leading him forcibly toward a nearby entrance to a small eatery, whose sign identified it as the Forty-Seventh Street Sandwich Shop.

As they entered the restaurant, the crowd outside began to disperse, losing interest quickly in the spectacle of the purple-faced man continuing to shout at a now-departed target. His ire suddenly unfocused, the man also seemed to lose interest rapidly, and he returned to his search through the contents of the trash basket. Tim, looking back through the window, felt a flood of relief as his pulse began to return to normal.

Mike, still pulling him by the sleeve, went to the end of a line which snaked up toward a deli counter behind which perspiring men were preparing sandwiches. "We had to get out of there, Tim. You couldn't have hurt the old guy just by bumping into him. He was anaesthetized. But never draw attention to yourself in this town. It just causes complications. Where are you from, anyway?"

"Bridgeport, Connecticut," replied Tim, still somewhat shaken.

"Well, that's not exactly the country," said Mike. "Did you go to school up there?"

"No, I went to Fordham."

"Fordham? For God's sake, that's right here in New York. You must've seen plenty of bums wandering around over there. Oh, wait a minute, I see ... You must think we have a higher class of bum over here on Park Avenue. Think you committed a faux pas in front of a sophisticated crowd, do you?"

Tim didn't reply, but Mike was right. He felt a little out of place here on Park Avenue, as if the passersby knew he did not belong.

Five minutes later, after having spent nearly two dollars apiece for moderately-thick deli sandwiches and sodas, they sat together on a low wall surrounding some plantings in front of one of the Park Avenue glass towers. Mike took three bites from his combination corn beef and pastrami. "So, what's the story?" he asked, chewing heartily. "Did they really give you something to work on, or just leave you reading the office procedure manual all morning?"

"No," said Tim, brightening at the thought that such an early assignment to a case might be a favorable sign. "They have me working on a case. Mr. Watson called me in this morning and told me one of the firm's clients had died over the weekend. He wants me to help him with the probate proceeding."

"Listen, Tim," interjected Mike. "Don't call him Mr.

Watson. Call him Rem. I'm sure that's what he told you to do, and that's what they want you to do. If you start calling him Mr. Watson, or even referring to him that way, you'll just be reminding him that you went to Fordham and are feeling inferior. He and the other partners may actually think of you that way, too, since BLT is one of the last of the dyed-in-the-wool white shoe firms. But it makes them ill at ease to have it come up. Act confident. Otherwise you're reminding them that they brought you in as cannon fodder during a slow hiring season."

"Thanks," Tim nodded, grateful for what he knew to be good advice, although uncomfortable to be discussing the subject all the same. "What do you mean by 'slow hiring season' and 'cannon fodder'?"

"Well, they hired you late, right?"

"Yeah, but is that something I should be worried about?"

"Not really. It's still a nice place to work and a great salary right off the bat, but what they really want is more of the same. More of the prep school Ivy Leaguers. More people like themselves. Sometimes they come up a little short in that department, but they still need warm bodies to do the work. So they hire some smart kids, like you and me. Pay us well and put an invisible label on us that says 'not for partnership, recycle after seven years from date of hire.'"

"Recycle?"

"Yeah, help us find a nice spot with a corporate client or a bank when the time comes for an honorable discharge."

"So I'm just cannon fodder?"

"Yeah, and so am I, but don't worry about it. BLT is a good place to be from one day, when you're looking for a job. Don't let it get you down."

"I won't. Anyway, it's way too early for me to think I'd even be good enough to make partner some day. But do they ever make exceptions?"

"Once in a great while, and I mean a very great while, they've made someone a partner who wasn't one of them.

There's Pappas in international and Steiner in tax, but like I said, that's rare. And only if they can't help it for some reason. That reason is always money, of course, but money alone won't do it. The person has to have some class and a big reputation. I mean look at Tom Quinn in the T & E department. He's been here forever, clients love him, the partners rely on him, and the courts respect him. But that's not enough, so no partnership. They let him stick around because his work generates revenue, and he doesn't complain."

Tim was getting a little lost.

"T & E Department? What's that?"

"Trusts and Estates, my man. The world of the rich and the privileged. In fact, it's the world where your first matter lives. So who died?" continued Mike, almost flippantly.

Tim was confused momentarily, thinking that Mike assumed his serious expression was the result of hearing that he was not on the "partnership track," but then he realized that Mike must be resuming their conversation about Tim's new case.

"Oh," said Tim. "You mean the estate I'm working on. A client named Reginald V. Simpson—"

"Simpson! The securities guy over at Trundle, Betts? He's been on the Securities and Exchange Commission's 'Ten Most Wanted' list for years."

"Really?" asked Tim. "He was a fugitive?"

Mike laughed. "I don't mean that list. I mean he was too smart for them. They practically ran up the white flag whenever they heard that he'd been retained by some Big Board company they'd decided to investigate. They'll probably send flowers to his funeral. How did he die?"

"He had some kind of an accident in his apartment. He hit his head on a table and bled to death. I don't really know much more about it yet," replied Tim.

"No kidding? That's a great case for you to get involved in right away," said Mike. "Simpson moved in some pretty heavy circles. We were all sure he was on his way to the Second Circuit this winter. Too bad you're only handling the probate proceeding. That's pretty dull stuff. If you hadn't shown up today, they would probably have asked a summer associate or a secretary to do it."

"Is it that easy?" asked Tim, somewhat hopefully. He was a little nervous about flubbing his very first assignment.

"Oh, yeah. They just fill out some forms and file them with the Will in the Surrogate's Court. Generally, everyone signs off and you have the thing probated in a week. It's like rolling off a log. Believe it or not, a few years ago, a senior estates partner at BLT drew up his own probate papers before he died. He left them in a folder in his desk for his secretary to find after he went. I guess even a week's delay from death to probate was too long for his professional pride."

"But aren't there ever any problems?" asked Tim. "What about all these stories you hear about probate contests?"

"They're very rare," said Mike. "Especially at big firms like ours. They're awfully careful with the drafting and signing of the Wills, for one thing. And most of the clients' families realize that it's better to save their strength to fight the Internal Revenue Service than to use it up early fighting with one another. Probate proceedings are pretty tame here. Go see Tom Quinn when you get back to the office. He's invaluable for all he knows about Surrogate's Court procedures, estate tax audits, and stuff like that."

Tim was reassured by the news that his first assignment would expose him to the affairs of one of the powerful members of the New York legal establishment, without at the same time subjecting him to a nerve-racking baptism by fire into the practice of law itself.

He should have known better.

9

TIM FELT UPLIFTED returning to the office, despite having been told he was "cannon fodder." The sensation intensified when he passed Miss Jones in the reception area.

"Good afternoon, Mr. O'Leary. Did you enjoy your lunch?" she asked with a friendly smile.

He smiled back at her, admiring her perfectly-featured face. "Yes, Miss Jones. Very much. Thank you."

Entering his office, he sat down and attacked the Simpson file with renewed vigor. He removed the last unread folder, marked "Assets," from the file and opened it. At once his insecurities returned.

A single page provided a succinct but impressive list of the assets of Reginald V. Simpson, Esq. Some he had apparently inherited and others had been the product of his own labors. The assets included a cooperative apartment on Manhattan's East Side, a summer residence in East Hampton, and a fishing and hunting cabin on a lake in the Adirondacks. A footnote indicated that another home, in Palm Beach, Florida, as well as numerous other assets, had been ceded to the second wife in the recent divorce action. The list of Reginald Simpson's assets continued by itemizing several categories of securities, cash accounts, family trusts, commercial real estate holdings, insurance, investment partnerships and a variety of other interests. In total, Simpson's estate was valued at over 50 million dollars.

Tim practically ran to Tom Quinn's office.

Quinn was an older man, probably in his early sixties. He had a large frame, close-cropped grey hair, and a prominent nose. He could almost be described as a man with rugged good looks, except that something was lacking, thought Tim. Perhaps that something was nothing more than the 20 by 20 corner office and partnership status that created an aura around men like Rem Watson. With a start, Tim realized that, in only half a day, he was already beginning to accept the subtle inferences of power that were so much a part of life at the offices of Bradford, Lord & Turner. He introduced himself, and sat down in the chair Quinn offered.

Quinn was obviously a man who accepted the fact that he was at BLT to work and not to socialize. After observing the briefest of social niceties, he got to the point.

"So, Tim, I assume they have assigned you to an estate. Whose?"

"A Mr. Simpson," said Tim. Then, remembering Mike's advice, he added, "Tom."

"Reginald V. Simpson?" asked Quinn, appearing somewhat surprised.

"Yes."

"When did *he* die?" inquired Quinn, sagging somewhat. His eyes became unfocused, as if this information were a signal that his turn was drawing that much closer.

"Just before the weekend, I think," replied Tim. "Rem Watson told me that they found the body only this morning, but that he had apparently been dead for several days. He had an accident in his apartment. Did you know him?"

"Yes, I did," Quinn responded dreamily, "Although not that well. Actually, Rex and I were law school classmates many years ago."

He sighed and laid his forearms on the desk, willing himself back to the business at hand. "Well, that is sad news. I suppose they gave this one to you knowing that it might upset me to be involved. Here is what you have to do."

For the next half hour, Quinn gave Tim a crash course in the mechanics of probating a Will in the State of New York, a process designed to prove that the document was valid before it was allowed to control the disposition of a deceased person's assets. First, a petition must be drawn. In it, the executor, which in this case was Morgan Guaranty Trust Company, would ask a court known as the Surrogate's Court to accept the Will as valid. The petition would also ask the court to give the executor the legal authority to take control of the assets, so that taxes and debts could be paid and the beneficiaries named in the Will could be given whatever had been provided for them. He informed Tim that the venerable Morgan Guaranty was the finest of the New York trust companies. He suggested that while Tim might find their trust officers a bit superior, especially in dealing with someone as green as Tim, their experience and expertise would nevertheless be an invaluable resource in his continuing professional development.

After indulging in this brief discourse on the virtues and vices of the iconic Morgan Guaranty, Quinn returned to his tutorial. The probate petition would reduce Reginald V. Simpson to his bare essentials: name, address, citizenship and date of death. It would identify his executor and next of kin, and advise the court of the date on which he had executed his Last Will and who had served as witnesses. It would also name those who were to receive something under the Will. Lastly, it would advise the court of the size of the estate, but since this information was only relevant to the fixation of the court filing fee the petition could simply say "over $1,000,000." At this level, the maximum filing fee of $150 would be due. The fact that this estate was 50 times that large would not have to be disclosed.

The other Court papers would be similarly brief and to the point. Affidavits must be filed which would be signed by the Will's witnesses, attesting to the fact that the Will was signed with due observance of the required formalities, that Mr. Simpson appeared to be of sound mind on that day, and that no one was holding a gun to his head or otherwise forcing him to do something he didn't want to do.

A notice would also be prepared for mailing to the lucky ones who would benefit under the Will if it were admitted to probate. This did not apply to the next of kin, or "distributees" as they were technically known. They were entitled to a more formal notification of the proceeding, since they would have received the entire estate if there had been no Will. Constitutional due process therefore gave them the right to contest the probate of this one if they believed it was invalid. As a practical matter, however, since family members were usually the primary beneficiaries under the Will, they generally waived this notification and consented to probate.

Quinn called this last document a "citation" and said that it was actually issued by the clerk of the court, although it was prepared by the executor's attorney. He said copies had to be delivered, by a process server if necessary, to the next of kin who had not signed waivers. It gave them an opportunity to come into the court on a date specified in the citation if they wanted to question the validity of the Will.

This reminded Tim of a provision in the copy of the Will which he had read earlier that day. It was a clause specifically disinheriting the late Mr. Simpson's brother Harold. Tim mentioned it to Quinn.

Quinn again seemed to be jolted, his jaw dropping like that of a prizefighter receiving a hard blow. Recovering quickly, he explained his surprise by reminding Tim that he had not been too close to Simpson's affairs, either personal or professional, in some time, but that this sounded like a recipe for a probate contest. Businesslike again, he voiced the opinion that, in cases of disinheritance, it was generally more prudent to make some provision for the "black sheep" and combine it with an "In Terrorem" clause.

Seeing Tim's puzzled expression, Quinn elaborated. Simpson's Will could have contained a bequest to his brother of, say, $100,000, not an insignificant sum obviously but only a tiny fraction of his massive estate. The Will would go on to say, however, that if the brother challenged the validity of the Will in an attempt to get more, and lost, the bequest would be revoked and he would get nothing. So he would have to choose between accepting the proffered bequest or risking it all by contesting probate.

In any event, since this approach had not been used here, there would probably be no point in asking Rex's brother Harold to sign a waiver. Instead, Tim should prepare the formal citation for issuance by the clerk of the court, so that it could be served on the estranged brother. In any case, Quinn opined, even if the brother might be inclined to consent to the probate of this Will, it would seem somewhat less than sporting to ask him to do so.

Quinn reached into a file cabinet next to his desk for the various Surrogate's Court forms which Tim would require. He slid them across his desk toward Tim, saying they should be used for preparing drafts, which would then be submitted to the steno pool so they could be typed up.

"Well, young man." Quinn crossed his hands in his lap and smiled. "I wish you the best of good fortune in this matter, and in your career as well. Rex and I started out together but, due perhaps to our differences in background as much as anything, he soon left me far behind. I think that I can assure you that we are a more enlightened society, and firm, today. I'm quite certain that if you apply yourself, and receive your reasonable share of luck, your career will be every bit as satisfying as you might wish."

Tim rose on this cue, and, thanking Tom, left his office with a new feeling of optimism.

"Oh, I almost forgot," called Quinn. Tim turned around. "When the papers have been prepared, signed and notarized, stop by to see Miss Tedesco. She supervises the file department. You'll need to requisition the original Will from the firm's vault so you can file it in court. You can't have a probate proceeding without a Will, after all," he added with a chuckle.

10

FOR THE REST OF THE AFTERNOON, Tim laboriously completed the various probate forms. He had to return to Quinn's office from time to time for help with one question or another. At 5:30, when Mike Green stopped by his office to say hello, the papers were finished.

"Well, how's Simpson coming?" Mike put his hands on his narrow hips while waiting for an answer, reminding Tim of the Planters Peanut man, only without the monocle and the top hat.

"Oh. Hi, Mike. Pretty well, thanks. Tom Quinn gave me a lot of help, and I have all of the probate forms filled out. By the way, how do I get them typed?" asked Tim.

Green pointed to the top drawer in Tim's desk. "You have requisition slips in there for just about everything you'll need around here. The ones that say 'Stenographic' are for ordering typing from the secretarial pool. Clip one of those to what you've filled out, add a clean set of forms for them to type on, write your name on the slip and drop the whole thing in the out box on your desk. One of those guys with the green blazers will pick it up when he makes his rounds. He'll drop it off at the steno pool when he goes by there. They should get it back to you by tomorrow afternoon. Ready to call it a day?"

"I guess so. The only other work I have to do is some research, and that can wait until tomorrow. Are you leaving?"

"Not yet. I was just on my way out to get some dinner. After that I'll be working tonight," answered Green. "We're trying to meet a deadline on some interrogatories. Big shareholder derivative action against Trans West Metals. Anyways, want to join me?"

"Sure," said Tim, remembering that Rick, the law school classmate who shared his apartment was still away on a post-bar exam vacation. He did not feel like eating alone tonight, at the end of the first day of his professional career. He found the requisition slips in his top drawer, asked Mike to give him a minute while he filled them out, and then attached them to the penciled drafts of the probate papers. After he placed them in his out box, he turned off the light in his office and walked down the hall with Mike toward the reception area and the elevators.

When they reached the elevators, a tall bespectacled young man was waiting for them.

"Tim, this is Ken Clark," said Green. "He's coming to dinner with us."

Tim reached out to shake Ken's hand. "Nice to meet you. Are you also an associate here?"

"One of our corporate types," interjected Mike before Clark could answer, "shepherding public offerings through the SEC to pad his pockets. Ken, meet Tim O'Leary, a new associate as of today. About to learn trusts and estates at the feet of our *eminence grise* Thomas Quinn."

"Good to meet you, too," smiled Ken, returning the handshake as they entered the elevator.

When they reached the street, the day was finally cooling, and the walk to a nearby early dinner restaurant was a pleasant one. The five o'clock crowd had apparently dispersed, and the jostling frenzy of the lunch hour had been replaced by an air of day's-end satisfaction as the early evening's pedestrians glided along Park Avenue.

Mike said they should get a little New York atmosphere to go with their dinner, so they headed over to Third Avenue and its legendary P.J. Clarke's, still in business 84 years after its opening in 1884. They were served by only moderately surly waiters, and the steaks and burgers ordered by Tim and Mike would have merited a standing ovation at Smokey's. Ken, after reading the menu with a raised eyebrow, ordered a salad, later describing it as "tolerable if one is in a hurry."

Tim enjoyed a feeling of comradeship and well-being as he listened to Mike and Ken (whose full name was Kensington, Tim would later learn) trade war stories about their recent experiences at the firm. In a particularly entertaining anecdote, Mike recounted the depredations committed by an unsavory adversary, the plaintiff's lead counsel in the Trans West Metals case.

"Last week, he told Judge Pierce that every judge on the Southern District bench, and every judge in the Federal court system for that matter, had to disqualify himself from the case. His argument? He had found out that the Federal judges' pension fund held shares of Trans West Metals. Later on in the hallway, he told me that he didn't really think his argument was so great. He said to look at the judges, it was obvious they were so old they had long since passed retirement age, and had no intention of ever collecting their pensions, anyway."

Tim and Ken laughed.

"But when Pierce asked him who would decide the case if all of the judges on the Federal bench were required to disqualify themselves, he was a little taken aback, since he had been so excited about the stir he might cause with his disqualification motion that he hadn't thought it through that far. Not to be caught short, though, he came right back at Judge Pierce, and without blinking an eye, he said 'Your honor, how about my brother-in-law? He's always wanted to be a judge, and his law practice has been a little slow lately. He has plenty of time on his hands.'"

Tim was so delighted to be a member of the group that he would probably have found any outlandish tale the others came up with to be believable if not funny, but this one was certainly the latter, if not the former. When he was finally able to stop laughing, he said he could never in his wildest dreams have the nerve to act this way in a courtroom. Had he thought about it, he might have wondered whether Mike was embellishing the story somewhat for his listeners. But Tim was on such a high from the day, the dinner and the fun, he wasn't about to over-analyze.

After they wrapped up with coffee, Ken rose from the table and handed Green his share of the tab. "I'd better get going if I want to nail down a good seat." As he said this, he seemed to have a brainstorm of some sort, and turned to Tim.

"Tim, perhaps you'd like to join me. I have an extra ticket to a concert I'm attending this evening. It's part of a Baroque festival being given by the Westminster Choral Society, at the Episcopal cathedral up in Morningside Heights."

Tim had no idea what Baroque music was, but he was anxious to continue his association with both Mike and Ken. He consented readily, and rose to join Clark after quickly settling his share of the check. He wished Mike good luck with his night's assignment.

"What's that lawyer's name, anyway?" he asked.

"Marty Green," snickered Mike.

"The same name as yours?"

Ken smiled. "No more holding out now, Mike. You have to fess up."

"He's my uncle," Mike confessed with a grin.

"Personality runs in the family." Ken elbowed Tim.

"He keeps telling me that if I act too smart in this case, he'll move to disqualify me also," said Mike. "I think he means it. The only thing he doesn't understand is that a move like that would only help me with the partners at BLT. I've always been a little bit suspect in their eyes, and when they found out I was related to the infamous Marty Green, they were appalled."

"Geez!" gasped Tim. "You have to go against your own uncle in court? And he's a lawyer like that to boot?"

"Oh, he's not that bad," said Mike. "I'll have to tell you about Uncle Marty's buddy Jack 'the Rabbit' Reardon some day. Now *he's* a real character. One time—"

"Uh, Mike?" interrupted Ken, who had started shifting his feet nervously.

"Oh, right. You guys had better get to the show. We'll save the Rabbit for some other time. Enjoy the music, Tim," he said with a wink.

Somewhat mysteriously, Tim thought.

11

KEN WAS OBVIOUSLY CONCERNED about the time. Tim had to hurry to keep up with him as they left the restaurant. Once outside, Ken rushed out onto Third Avenue and hailed a Checker Cab heading uptown. It swerved to the curb with a squealing of brakes, and Ken and Tim hopped in. "John the Divine," he barked to the cabbie, and then turned to Tim to educate him on the "exquisite" sounds they were about to enjoy.

"Joan who, sir?" It was the cabbie, who was obviously not familiar with this particular individual, much less where she lived (or, he might be thinking, performed).

"Oh my goodness, driver, Mr. Nicholas is it?" Clark tried to decipher the name of the cabbie from the photo license affixed to the partition behind the front seat.

"Niculescu, sir, Danut Niculescu. Romanian. Can call me Danny."

"Well, Danny, we're not going to see someone named Joan. We'd like to go to a church up in Morningside Heights, a cathedral."

"Oh. Sorry. My English not so good yet. Where is this catedrala?"

"Quite all right, Danny. Your command of the language is commendable. The Cathedral of Saint John the Divine is located at One Hundred Twelfth and Amsterdam. Now we're a bit late, so I'd appreciate your getting us there as quickly as possible."

"Now talking my language, sir. Hold on to hats!"

Tim and Ken were thrown back in their seats as the cab flew up Third Avenue.

They arrived in less than 10 minutes. Tim offered to split the fare, but Ken waved him off.

"My treat, Tim. This evening's on me. You're going to love it."

They went inside the Cathedral, a stunning Gothic structure with a massive, circular stained-glass window above the main entrance. Clark hurried up the center aisle, and found available seating only a few rows from the front of the church. Risers had been set up on the altar for the performers.

They sat down in the wooden pew, and Ken finally relaxed, spending the next 15 minutes reciting the history of the unique musical genre of which this evening's performance was a part. Johann Sebastian Bach and George Frideric Handel, whom Clark referred to as two "giants" in the Baroque movement, had apparently been born during the same year, 1685. Handel moved to London in 1712, which was about the time Bach composed one of his first cantatas, and the full flowering of their respective musical geniuses began in earnest. Tonight was one of a series of presentations of the work of these two men. The Choral Society would perform a 1724 Bach cantata thought to be derived from what Ken described as the "lost cantata of 1718," which had been composed by Bach in someplace called Kothen exactly 250 years earlier. This, in Clark's opinion, added special significance and additional excitement to the evening's performance.

Tim took a deep breath, starting to feel a bit groggy from the information overload.

The small orchestra which played with the Choral Society's choir, Clark went on, would be playing on replicas of original Baroque instruments, which had a pitch somewhat different than that of modern musical instruments. In all, every effort would be made to faithfully reproduce the sound of three centuries ago. A sound that, Clark noted sadly, was not much in vogue these days.

In the final few minutes before the performance began, Tim's eyes wandered over the interior of the marvelous cathedral, following its vaulted arches as they gracefully rose to their meeting places high overhead. He looked with awe at the majestic detail that was everywhere, so typical of many older churches and so beautifully expressed in the structure where he now sat.

At 8:00 p.m. precisely, the performers having taken their places, the concert began. Tim was enthralled. The almost unreal sounds of the Baroque instruments flowed through the church, immersing but not assaulting Tim's senses with the haunting strains of another time. He felt that this must be the ecstasy of New York at its best—a place with unlimited opportunities for exploration and happiness, where life was good and being young and part of it even better.

At the end of the first 45 minutes, his back started to stiffen up a bit. Just a little at first, but enough to divert his attention from the music. He attempted to adjust his position to relieve the nagging discomfort. Furtively, he stole a glance at his companion, who appeared to be in an almost mystical trance, his lips barely rising in a slight smile of contented refinement. Ashamed of his own mundane concerns, Tim refocused his attention on the performers as they continued their production of the lovely, haunting music.

30 minutes later, his back began to cramp, muscles knotting further with every slight adjustment he made in his position. Again, his eyes wandered. Guiltily at first, but less so as his conscience was salved by the appearance of other heads nodding gently, other eyes discretely closing. Was that heaviness of breathing he thought he heard a sleep-induced one?

Were those yawns? Others must be afflicted with his weakness of flesh, his undisciplined mind, he concluded, but his guilt would not completely release its hold.

The music continued, its quaint beauty still evident. The lengthy solos and exuberant choruses evoked memories of incense and the rustle of vestments. Grasping for a second wind, Tim consulted the libretto to better understand the words being sung, only to find that most of the lines were being sung over and over again, sometimes two, three or more times, by the choir, whom he now feared might finally reach the end of the work, only to repeat it again in its entirety. He felt panicky, trapped, his back a mass of pain, screaming for release and relief. His watch, which at times he was certain had stopped, now showed two hours to have passed since the performance had begun. With no end in sight, not if they kept repeating those lines.

Then, suddenly, gloriously as if from heaven, the finale rose simultaneously from his libretto and the choir's throats. Tim's spirits soared with the voices of the tired but pride-bursting performers. His heart filled with the flooding certainty that no matter how many times they might repeat these last few lines, the end was near at hand. Over and over, and around and through, the finale they went. Until, exhausted and happy, the choir and the instrumentalists repeated the last line for the last time, held that last note for just one extra breathless moment of triumph—and stopped.

No one cheered harder than Tim.

12

TIM'S SECOND DAY ON THE JOB at BLT, as he was already calling it, began with the phone ringing.

"Mr. O'Leary, this is Greg Trout from JP Morgan. I'm the trust officer assigned to the Simpson Estate. I hear you're working on the probate papers."

Tim remembered Mike Green's admonition regarding first names. Assuming that what was good enough for Rem Watson must certainly be good enough for him, he replied, "My name is actually Tim."

"Your name is actually Timothy J. O'Leary, according to my records," laughed Trout patronizingly, "but I would be happy to call you Tim if you'd like, so long as you call me Greg. Now, when can we get together on those probate papers?"

"They're being typed up. Tom Quinn said he'll review them as soon as they come back from the steno pool, so they should be ready by this afternoon," Tim answered, pleased to be ready to comply with this first request for his professional work product. "Would you—"

"Good," cut in Trout. "Give me a call when you have

them. Maybe we can sign them up today at my office. I'd like to get this rolling as quickly as possible, before that no-account brother Harold starts thinking of ways to cause trouble. Talk to you later." Trout hung up.

Tim busied himself in the firm's paneled library for the rest of the morning, working on some small research jobs he'd been assigned by other, more senior associates the prior afternoon. At lunchtime, he ate again with Mike Green, who this time had a number of associates, including Ken Clark, in tow. Tim enjoyed himself, but politely refused Ken's invitation to another Baroque concert being held at a different church that evening.

When he returned to his office, the probate papers were on his desk. He pored through them with enthusiasm, enjoying the satisfaction of creating legal documents for the first time as an attorney. He was proud of the fact that he could verify each of the statements he had made in these papers by reference to the materials he had reviewed the day before, but he was probably prouder of the neatness of the typing that gave the documents such an impressive appearance. He picked up the phone and called Tom Quinn.

"I have the typed probate papers, Tom. Would you like to look them over?"

"Sure, Tim. I need something from the file room. Why don't I come by your office on the way so we can get them out this afternoon?"

Five minutes later, Quinn tapped politely on Tim's door.

"Now a good time, Tim?"

"Absolutely, Tom. Here they are." Tim handed the Simpson probate papers to Quinn, who sat down and began to look them over, occasionally checking portions against the materials in the Simpson file, which was on Tim's desk. Several minutes later, he looked up.

"Excellent. Good work."

Tim was thrilled. "Thanks, Tom, and thanks for your help. I'll call Greg Trout and let him know they're ready."

"Good. Now I'd better get moving." He rose and left.

Tim dialed Trout at Morgan Guaranty. He was feeling more like a lawyer every minute.

"Trout."

"Greg, this is Tim O'Leary at Bradford, Lord & Turner. How are you?"

"Just fine, Tim. No change from this morning. Probate papers ready?"

"Yes, they are," he replied, trying to speak with an assertiveness consistent with his new professional confidence. "I can bring them to you now if you'd like."

"Yes, please do. My office is at 23 Wall."

"Okay. I should be there in half an hour." Hanging up, Tim put the papers into a new file set up for the Simpson Estate. Before leaving the office, he placed the file into a briefcase Marge had surprised him with on their last night together in Bridgeport.

When he reached the street, and started the short walk to the Lexington Avenue subway's 42nd Street station, it was stifling as usual. Heavy looking white clouds were beginning to build up and the steamy sky was filled with a white glare. As he looked up, he again admired the beautiful buildings that lined the street.

Park Avenue's gleaming new office towers had been constructed in the 1950s and 1960s as a haven for the banks, law firms, brokerage houses and accounting firms which, along with other businesses in the financial community, were beginning to flee the aging and decaying Wall Street area. The rush to abandon New York City's apartments for houses in the comfortable Westchester and Connecticut suburbs had made Park Avenue's Grand Central Terminal a dropping off point each morning for thousands of executives and professionals. Few of them cared to then board the Lexington Avenue subway for the hot, crowded, stuffy ride to Wall Street that stole another 20 minutes each way from their already shrinking days. So they started to find fault with the midday darkness cast over the Financial District's narrow streets by the shadows of its tall buildings, its inaccessibility to vehicular traffic, and its lack of better restaurants. One by one, firms were beginning to yield to the urgings of their younger members and were signing leases uptown, especially on Park Avenue, with its trendy shops, upscale restaurants, abundant sunlight and, especially, its Grand Central Station.

Other areas had also begun to benefit from the northward migration. Fifth Avenue already boasted a number of impressive structures, and was adding its share of newer ones, the General Motors Building being the most noteworthy. The Rockefeller Center area, only a few subway stops from Penn Station, was proving to be a magnet for commuters from Long Island.

But Bradford, Lord and Turner was something of a pioneer among the old line banks and law firms, most of which had stayed on Wall Street. Morgan Guaranty Trust Company was one of them, still occupying its storied structure at 23 Wall Street, whose exterior walls remained pockmarked with the damage inflicted by an anarchist's bomb in 1920.

Tim got off the subway at the Wall Street station and took the escalator to the street level, finding himself in the lobby of the Irving Trust building, another landmark with its One Wall Street address. Once outside, after glancing briefly at still another historic structure across the street—Trinity Church—he turned toward 23 Wall and the office of Greg Trout.

Trout was sitting at a polished desk nearly covered with neatly stacked papers. Although his desk was located in an open area, there were no others near his, and a low partition had been erected to one side to produce some measure of privacy. Trout was probably somewhere between 45 and 50, and streaks of grey were beginning to infiltrate his straight black hair. He had no more patience for small talk when met in person than he had had on the phone, and Tim was beginning to suspect that Trout resented the instant parity between them which had resulted from Bradford, Lord & Turner's assignment of Tim to the Simpson Estate. Trout had obviously been around for awhile, and it looked as if he did not take kindly to being burdened with these lowly and inexperienced associates assigned by the major firms to his estates. Tim, hoping his suspicions were unfounded, sat and opened his briefcase.

"Here they are. Tom Quinn looked through them after they were prepared, so I think they should be all right. I know you will want to review them also, of course," ventured Tim, more tentatively than he would have liked.

"Thank you, I shall," replied Trout, somewhat curtly. He lowered his glasses to the end of his nose and began to closely scrutinize the documents. For the next fifteen minutes there was no conversation, the only significant sound being the crackle of each paper when Trout turned it over onto his desk after completing his inspection. Finally, when he had finished, he looked up at Tim and begrudged him a half-smile.

"Well, you may not know much about probating a Will," Trout commented, "but at least you had the sense to ask someone who does. These papers are fine. Do you have the Will?"

"No, it's in the office safe," said Tim, not certain whether to classify Trout's comments as positive or negative. "I planned to get it out when I was ready to file the probate papers in the Surrogate's Court."

"The bank will need copies for its files and the beneficiaries," lectured Trout in what must have been his best professorial tone.

Tim cringed.

"And your firm will require them for tax and accounting proceedings, as well as for its internal purposes. Please don't forget to make at least a dozen copies from the original before you file it in the Surrogate's Court, from whence only certified copies may be obtained, at the extortionary rate of a dollar a page, for every blasted one of them."

"Okay," said Tim, scribbling a note to himself. "I'm sorry I didn't think of that earlier. I can bring you your copies tomorrow when I go out to file the papers in court."

"I have a better idea," said Trout. "Why don't you call your office while I'm signing these for the bank? Ask them to pull the Will from the safe and start making the copies. They will know not to remove the staples from the original, as perhaps you do not, assuming the Will is stapled, although I suspect not. My experience with Bradford Lord has been that they bind their Wills with ribbon and then seal them at the execution ceremony—a procedure quite fitting to the solemnity of the document. In any event, they can use a messenger to bring my copies down here tomorrow while you're attending to more important things, like getting proof of service of this notice of probate completed and executed." Trout flourished the notice before Tim, who blushed. He realized that Trout was suggesting he had neglected to execute an affidavit stating that a copy of the notice had been mailed to Theodore Bracken, letting him know that Simpson's Will had been offered for probate.

"But Greg, that notice says the Will has been filed and the probate proceeding has been started. That won't be the case until we file the petition in the court." Tim did his best to suppress a triumphant smile.

"That's where experience trumps the world of the classroom, Tim," intoned Trout, not a little condescendingly. "The clerks won't accept the probate papers unless that affidavit is signed and notarized. I suppose they assume the notice will arrive at its destination after the filing, making the notice truthful, albeit somewhat retroactively. 'Nunc pro tunc,' as it were." He settled back into his chair contentedly, having put yet another overpaid young greenhorn in his place, flaunting his knowledge of legal jargon in the process. He picked up the telephone and began to dial.

Tim was unsure of whether he felt more annoyed or embarrassed. He reached over and took the telephone from Trout, who thrust it across the desk after first dialing the law firm's number, lest that task was also beyond Tim's capabilities. Tim was connected to Alice Tedesco, and asked her to obtain Reginald Simpson's Will from the office safe so that copies could be made. She said she would get to it right away. Before hanging up, she asked him where he was calling from in case she might have any questions. All very efficient.

Tim hung up and watched Trout sign the papers, and then squeeze the bank's raised seal onto them. After that, he applied a variety of rubber stamps to indicate his name, title, address, and some other information Tim's squinting eyes couldn't make out. Trout seemed to be enjoying himself. When he had finished, he looked up at Tim.

"Well, Morgan Guaranty is on board. It looks like all you have to do is pick up the original Will, mail the notice of probate to Mr. Bracken, sign the affidavit saying that you've done so, and then run the whole package down to the Surrogate's Court later this afternoon or first thing in the morning." He paused. "By the way, I hope I haven't offended you about the affidavit. This is a very precise business."

Tim doubted the sincerity of the apology. He suspected that Trout's superiors might look unkindly on making enemies, however insignificant they might be, at Bradford, Lord. But he was about to accept it anyway, when the telephone rang.

Trout picked it up, listened for a moment, and then handed it to Tim.

"It's your office," he said.

Tim took the telephone and held it to his ear, still looking at Trout.

"Mr. O'Leary?" It was Alice Tedesco.

"Yes, Miss Tedesco?" Timothy kept looking at Trout, still composing his answer.

"Mr. O'Leary, the Will is gone!"

Not understanding, but alarmed by the urgency of her

tone, Tim looked down at the phone's mouthpiece. "What do you mean gone? Where is it?"

"It's gone," she wailed. "The Will is gone. We don't have it!"

13

REM WATSON STEAMED. Miss Tedesco fretted. Tom Quinn seemed calm enough, but Austin Chamberlain, the young estates partner who had joined them in Watson's office, did not. Watson's secretary sat in the corner, taking notes. Tim himself couldn't help feeling somewhat excited by the crisis.

The meeting had been called for this morning as soon as Tim returned from Greg Trout's office and told Watson about the missing Will. Watson, stunned, had started making phone calls, telling each person he called to be in his office at nine the next morning. He had peremptorily brushed aside their requests to be excused from the meeting due to other commitments.

Now Watson paced his Persian carpet like Wellington at Waterloo, chastising his subordinates for their early mistakes, and mobilizing them for the crucial battles ahead. His command presence was impressive.

"Let me tell all of you right away that I consider this to be a very serious problem and, just as important, a very embarrassing one," he began. "First of all, it's no picnic probating a missing Will under the best of circumstances, but it can be damn near impossible when there's a contest. I don't need to remind you that this Will disinherits Rex Simpson's brother, and he's proven himself to be a troublemaker before."

Chamberlain, who looked to be in his late thirties, let out an acknowledging sigh.

"Secondly," said Rem, "Rex was an influential and well known man. The newspapers are going to love having something interesting to write about his probate proceeding, so we stand very little chance of having our sloppiness remain a secret around this town once the documents are filed in the Surrogate's Court. All right, let's talk. Miss Tedesco?"

She practically fell off her chair, of which she had been using only a few inches anyway. Tim had never seen anyone so pale, except perhaps at wakes, and those individuals had not been the ones sitting on the chairs.

"Yes, Mr. Watson," she gasped, on the verge of bursting into tears. Tim noticed that the first name rule did not apply to file department supervisors.

"Miss Tedesco, tell us again exactly what happened from the first time you heard that Mr. Simpson had signed a new Will."

"Oh, Mr. Watson, I know I wasn't there when you called that day." She trembled noticeably. "It was Mary Torino's birthday and we all went out to lunch together. We were a little late getting back, but we only do that a few times a year and—" She stopped abruptly and shrank back into her chair as Watson raised his hand impatiently.

"Miss Tedesco," he interjected, "my concern is not with your friend's birthday party. I want to find out what happened to Mr. Simpson's Will. Can you get to that, please?"

"Oh, yes, certainly, of course, Mr. Watson." Having to discuss her late return from the birthday lunch had obviously been a major concern for her. Watson's lack of interest was a relief. She was almost relaxed as she continued.

"When I came back to the file department after lunch that day, there was a message on my desk. It said that I was to come to your office, Mr. Watson, to pick up a new Will. So I came right away and you gave me a Will that you said Mr. Simpson had signed. I took it from you and went back to my department, where I made four copies, as I always do when a bank is executor. One for the client's file, one for the client, one for the bank and one for the partner in charge of the matter. That was you in this case, Mr. Watson," she said brightly.

"Yes, Miss Tedesco, I realize that. Please continue." He paused for a moment, seeing the look of hurt on her face, and added, "You're being very helpful."

"Well, Mr. Watson," she continued, mollified, "after I made the copies, I opened the office Will safe and put Mr. Simpson's Will in there, under 'S.'"

"When did you next try to locate the Will?" Watson asked.

"Just yesterday, Mr. Watson, when Mr. O'Leary called from the bank. My master list showed Mr. Simpson's Will as being in the safe, but when I opened the safe to take it out, it wasn't there. At first, I wasn't too concerned. I always try to keep the Wills in alphabetical order, but we have so many Wills with names that start with 'S' that I thought maybe I had put Mr. Simpson's Will in the wrong place in the 'S' section. So I looked through the whole section, but I still couldn't find it. I was really upset. I called Mr. O'Leary right away. I ... I'm sorry."

Now she did start to cry, sobbing and gasping and repeating the words "I'm sorry" over and over.

Tim felt compassion for her. He realized that she must have suffered a sleepless night in anticipation of having to attend this meeting, and was probably so distraught by the time it began that it was only a matter of time until she began to come apart, as she was doing now. He felt that he should do something to comfort her, to let her know that not everyone here was as self-assured as Rem Watson, and that he, too, would want to run back into the file room and bawl if he were in her shoes.

But he remained silent. He still felt more like an observer than a participant in these events. It was Tom Quinn who came to Miss Tedesco's rescue.

"Now, now, Alice," soothed the old gentleman, rising from his chair and walking to her side. He stooped from the waist and placed one arm protectively around her shoulders, patting her clenched fists with his other hand.

"We all know you did nothing wrong here. Mr. Watson is just trying to establish a sequence of events, so that we may all approach the resolution of this problem in an orderly manner. Your attention to the details of office procedure is well known in this firm, my dear. Almost legendary, I would say. Without your help, I am afraid we would be at a serious disadvantage in this matter."

As Quinn spoke, Miss Tedesco calmed perceptibly. After a few minutes, Quinn nodded to Watson that he might continue with his inquiries.

Watson had been half sitting on, half leaning against, the edge of his desk while Tom Quinn ministered to Alice. He was patient, not antagonistic, but clearly determined to continue with the business at hand the moment this distraction subsided. On Quinn's signal, he gently pushed off from the desk.

"Feeling better, now, Miss Tedesco?" he inquired, more to regain her attention than to suggest that a negative answer might be in any way acceptable.

"Yes, Mr. Watson, I'm all right now. Thank you," she responded, looking up at him with eyes that were still shining with the dampness of her tears.

"Good, let's continue then," he said, the tone of his voice making it evident that no further hysterics would be tolerated. "Have you searched the entire safe for the Will?"

"No, Mr. Watson, just the 'S' section. I would never have filed his Will outside of that section," she replied with uncharacteristic firmness, the order of the Will safe clearly a matter of professional pride to her. Tim doubted that Rem was going to find Reginald Simpson's Will in the "R" section.

"Well, check it anyway, will you?" said Watson, "Maybe someone else moved it by mistake."

Of course, thought Tim, Alice Tedesco must take vacations, get sick, play hooky from time to time. Someone else must have access to the Will safe to cover for her when she was not in the office. Why hadn't he thought of that? It was simple, but it was lawyerly, and he was supposed to be a lawyer. Tim realized the grandeur of his surroundings at the firm had generated a growing confidence that two and one half days in the practice of law did not justify. He hoped Watson didn't ask him a question.

"All right, Mr. Watson," he heard Miss Tedesco say. "I will go through the entire safe today."

"Good," replied Watson. "By the way, who does have access to the Will safe?"

"Well, there's myself, of course," she answered. "And also Lydia Washington, the assistant supervisor of the file department. Then there's Mr. Bennett, the office administrator, and of course all of the firm's partners—I think there are thirty-six of them right now. That's about it. Oh, and Mr. Quinn. He has access also."

"My Lord," gasped Watson. "That amounts to forty people! Do you maintain a written record of who goes in and out of the safe?"

"Yes, I do, Mr. Watson." Again on familiar ground, Miss Tedesco spoke with greater assurance. "I leave a daily log book next to the safe at all times. Anyone accessing the safe must sign the book on that day's page and also write the name of any client whose Will or trust agreement is deposited or removed. I check the log every day to see which Wills and trusts have been put in or taken out. I use that information to update my master list of the safe's contents. Most of the Wills that are taken out of the safe aren't coming back. They're going to be probated or returned to the client. But sometimes that's not the case, and then I keep after the person who took it out to make sure it comes back."

"Do many of the partners use the safe?" interjected Watson.

"No, Mr. Watson, just the estates partners mostly. And they usually call me and ask me to do it for them. They hardly ever come down themselves," answered Miss Tedesco. "But, Mr. Watson?" She looked uncertain as to whether or not to broach a possibly sensitive subject.

"Yes?" Watson's tone indicated that there was no room for holding back, not until this matter was cleared up.

"Sometimes the partners don't make the entries in the log the way they're supposed to. You know, if they're in a rush or something, they just take a Will and leave. I usually chase after them and get the information if I'm there, but if I'm not, the other girls are a little shy about ... well, you know, bothering a partner."

I'll bet, thought Tim, imagining the reaction of one of the more imperious partners to one of the office twerps telling him to get the hell back into the file room to report what he had taken.

"Oh, Christ," Watson said. He turned to Chamberlain, who had not participated verbally in the meeting up to that point, but whose attention had nevertheless been directly focused on Watson throughout.

"Austin, no matter what happens here, I would like you to see that procedures for the safekeeping of Wills by this office are tightened up."

"Right, Rem, I'll run that by the other partners right away. We'll crystallize their input and have a memo for you by week's end with some preliminary recommendations." He was scribbling furiously on a yellow pad as he spoke.

Tim thought he detected Watson rolling his eyes slightly (was he reacting to the suggestion that the criminals were best suited to eradicate the crime?). As quickly as it came, however, this merest of hints of disapproval of one of his fellow elect disappeared, and Watson again addressed Alice.

"Miss Tedesco, I would like to clear up one small item and then I will let you go. You mentioned that both the partners and Mr. Quinn have access to the Will safe, but you referred only to the partners when you said that some of the attorneys have been removing Wills without making the required log entries. Did you make that distinction consciously?"

"Of course, Mr. Watson."

"Why?"

"Because Mr. Quinn would never do something like that. He's very good about following procedures and cooperating with the staff. Everyone in the office knows that." She smiled warmly at Quinn, who responded with a benign smile of his own.

"All right, Miss Tedesco. Thank you," Rem nodded. "When you've finished your search of the safe, please report your findings to Mr. O'Leary. Also check the Will master list to see if Mr. Simpson's Will was ever removed from the safe during his lifetime. Oh, and Mr. Chamberlain will presumably be in contact with you eventually regarding an updating of procedures for the Will safe." He concluded by nodding to Miss Tedesco, apparently indicating she could leave, which she did.

Watson turned back to Chamberlain, who was taking more notes than Watson's secretary. "Austin?"

Chamberlain looked up instantly. "Yes, Rem?"

"Austin, what are the prospects in the probate proceeding if we're not able to find the original Will?"

"There should be no problem, Rem," Chamberlain responded eagerly. He reminded Tim of a bright young lieutenant, delivering a report on tactics memorized from his field manual. It sounded good enough, but it didn't instill the same confidence as General Watson's polish and command presence or Sergeant Major Quinn's battle-hardened competence.

"The law presumes revocation of a missing Will only where the original was last known to be in the possession of the testator," Chamberlain continued, erect in his chair.

"That's not the case here, of course, since preliminary indications are that we were the ones who lost the Will."

Watson winced, and Tim thought he heard Quinn suppress a chuckle. "Let's reserve judgment on that for the time being, Austin. Go on."

"The burden will be on us to prove the contents of the Will, Rem, but that won't be a problem here. I drafted it, you reviewed it and watched him sign it, and we have a Xerox copy that was made right afterwards, so we're good on proving the contents of the Will as we are required to do in these cases by Section 1407 of the Surrogate's Court Procedure Act. And once those technical hurdles are met, we will of course have no difficulty in proving that Rex Simpson was competent and that the Will reflects his intentions as to the disposition of his estate. I can see no reason why we should encounter any difficulty in probating it, even if we never do find the original."

His dissertation concluded, Chamberlain smiled and settled back into his chair, pleased to have been given the opportunity to demonstrate his erudition.

"Thank you, Austin," said Watson. "That's very reassuring. I think our best course of action is beginning to clarify itself. Tim?"

Tim jumped. It was his turn, but he wasn't ready. The others had had information, ideas. He had nothing. No matter what Watson might want to solicit from him, he was sure it wasn't there. He was sure that Austin was waiting for him to demonstrate the silliness of the hiring partners' tendency to address temporary manpower shortages by venturing beyond the Ivy League to the more pedestrian law schools in the hinterlands. When Tim looked in his direction, however, Chamberlain was again engrossed in his note taking and paying him no attention whatsoever. Less self-consciously, Tim looked back at Watson, only then realizing from Watson's expression that he had kept him waiting overlong for a reply.

"Oh. I'm sorry, Rem," said Tim, uncomfortable again.

"Tim, I want you to put together a whole new set of papers for the probate proceeding. If this Will stays lost, we have to proceed under the provision Austin mentioned, and some of your work will have to be revised. Tom can help you with that."

"Yes, Rem," said Tim, nodding at Watson and then at Quinn.

"But either way," Rem warned, "I want to be able to move on this by Friday. I don't like the idea of Harold Simpson sitting around concocting schemes while we review the guest list for Mary Torino's birthday party. Tom?"

"Yes, Rem?" Tom replied in his usual courtly and gentlemanly manner. Quinn, a man with neither hope of rising nor fear of plunging, seemed eternally placid. Tim remembered his father's assertions that "when you stops goin' up, you starts comin' down," and looked forward to telling him about this exception to the rule.

"Tom, I hope you can spare a few minutes for Tim on this. I know we've been keeping your calendar chockablock lately, but this may get a little dicey for Tim if we keep changing the scenario on him as we go along."

"No need for an apology, Rem. We all share your interest in the reputation of the firm. And it has always been my pleasure to assist young men like Tim as they begin their careers."

Quinn might be too good to be true, but Tim couldn't get enough of him.

"You're a rock, Tom, and you know we appreciate it," responded Watson with sincerity. "Well, Tim, there you have it. Get us two sets of probate papers and we'll decide which one to use when Miss Tedesco tells us whether or not we have Rex Simpson's Will."

Watson turned back to the others. "Gentlemen, I think that should do it for now. Thank you."

They rose to leave the office, except for Chamberlain, who busied himself briefly with the completion of his note taking, and then bustled over to Watson and congratulated him on the manner in which he had conducted the meeting.

"I think you've put out the fire on this one, Rem. You'll have us in and out of probate and Morgan Guaranty administering the estate before Harold Simpson wakes up from his latest hangover." As he said this, he brushed lightly past Tom Quinn, who had risen from his chair and was turning to leave. Austin didn't excuse himself.

Tim noticed Quinn's face tighten slightly, but otherwise there was no sign of resentment from this stolid gentleman as he plodded from the room. If anything, he seemed to be smiling.

14

LATER THAT DAY, the blistering heat which had scorched the city all week fed the haze overhead to unsustainable proportions. The sky darkened ominously and inexorably, and Tim looked up from the papers he was preparing to see wide bolts of lightning begin smashing into New Jersey across the river.

He was enjoying watching the approaching storm from the safety of his glassed-in shelter when he heard a soft tapping on his office door. He turned to see Alice Tedesco just as the flash of a nearby lightning bolt illuminated her eerily in the doorway.

"Mr. O'Leary," she said hesitantly, not crossing the threshold.

"Yes?" he replied, amused by the drama of the scene as he envisioned it might appear in an old black and white movie, with the lightning flashes reflecting off the saucer-eyed employee.

"Mr. Simpson's Will is not in the safe. I've searched it from top to bottom."

A clap of thunder rocked the room and startled him out of his reverie. He tried not to laugh, doubting he could explain to Miss Tedesco how perfect she might have been for the part in his imagined movie. Besides, the timing of the thunder had unnerved him.

He tried to act businesslike. "Do you have any idea who might have removed the Will, Miss Tedesco?"

"Well, Mr. O'Leary, when I finished searching the safe, I went through the log book to see if anyone had ever signed the Will out." She paused as lightning flashed again.

"And?"

"Mr. Chamberlain did."

Another crash of thunder.

"Mr. Chamberlain? Why would he do that?"

"I don't know, Mr. O'Leary. He signed it out on July eighteenth and never signed it back in. Then later the same day, he signed out Mr. Simpson's old Will, but almost right away he signed that one back in."

Tim was getting jumpy from the flickering of the lightning and the crashing of the thunder, as he wrestled to absorb the inexplicable information being conveyed by Alice Tedesco. Why would Austin Chamberlain remove the Will? The file indicated that Rem had been the one who was primarily responsible for the firm's dealings with Simpson. Chamberlain had merely drafted the Will. And why had Chamberlain taken the old Will and then returned it so quickly? Moreover, why hadn't he mentioned any of this information during the meeting called by Rem?

"Miss Tedesco. Alice. Do you mind if I call you by your first name?"

"Oh no, Mr. O'Leary. Please do," she answered, with more than a trace of eagerness.

"Good. Well, Alice, would you mind sitting down here for a minute while I check the Simpson file? Something about this doesn't make sense. And you can call me Tim, by the way."

"Certainly, Mr. O'Leary. Tim, I mean." She demurely sat down, smiling as she did so. "My, what a storm this is."

Tim turned back to look at his window just as the rain arrived, a few large drops striking the glass at first and then a torrent, exploding against the window and cascading off in sheets. It was an exciting backdrop for the mystery surrounding the disappearance of Simpson's Will. The presence of Alice, a witness to some of the key events, added to the intrigue. Tim opened the file with what he hoped was a sufficient air of gravity.

"Let's see, Alice, I remember something I saw in the correspondence file on Monday. Here it is. Mr. Watson wrote a letter to Mr. Simpson on July eighteenth, sending him a copy of his new Will. But the letter says the original of the old Will was also enclosed, at Mr. Simpson's request, since he wanted to destroy it. So how could Mr. Chamberlain have signed that one back in?"

"Well, he did," she answered a bit petulantly.

"But I remember you saying at the conference this morning that you had checked your master list and it showed that Mr. Simpson's Will was in the safe."

"I did, but I didn't notice that the date was the date of the old Will. I only realized that a few minutes ago when I looked at the daily logs and saw that it was Mr. Simpson's old Will that should have been in the safe—the one Mr. Chamberlain marked back in right after he took it out."

"In that case I had better call Mr. Watson and tell him, hadn't I? Thanks for your help. I'll let you know what we find out, if you'd like."

"Oh, I would, Tim. This is exciting! Things can get very boring down in the file room." Alice got up to leave.

Tim dialed Rem's extension. As Alice departed, she smiled over her shoulder, and turned the corner into the corridor just as Watson came on the line.

"Yes?" Watson's tone was neither imperious nor uncivil, just indicative of his certainty that the caller must have a good reason for interrupting whatever he was doing.

"Rem, this is Tim O'Leary."

"What's the latest?"

"Alice Tedesco has confirmed that the Will is not in the safe, and she found out something else that I don't understand. The log shows that Austin Chamberlain took Mr. Simpson's old and new Wills out of the safe on July eighteenth, but that he returned only the old one. Could that be?"

"Oh, for Christ's sake, that's impossible. I sent the old Will back to Rex. I remember very well. I asked Austin to get it from the Will safe for me and he brought the wrong one—the new one. So I sent him back and he got the old one instead, and I sent it to Rex."

"Alice says it was the old one he marked down in the log as a return. She seemed pretty certain," replied Tim.

"All right, I'll call Austin and get back to you." Watson abruptly hung up.

For the next fifteen minutes, Tim halfheartedly addressed himself to an affidavit he was preparing, at Tom Quinn's suggestion, regarding the absence of the original Will. The affidavit stressed the fact that Rex Simpson had never been in possession of the Will, and therefore could not be presumed to have destroyed it. More often than once, he caught himself staring through the window at the now-clearing western sky, and imagined what might happen if the wrong Will had been sent to Rex Simpson.

The phone rang again. It was Rem.

"Tim, Austin's here. He remembers quite clearly that he returned the new Will to the safe. He's checked the log and he realizes that he marked the old one back in by mistake. I talked to my secretary also, and she confirms my recollection that it was the old Will we sent to Rex. Your affidavit can safely say that the new Will was never delivered to the client."

"Well, I guess that settles it. Thanks, Rem." Tim hung up and resumed his drafting of the affidavit, concluding that there wasn't much intrigue to the matter after all, but somewhat disappointed that he hadn't been asked to pursue it further. By afternoon's end, he had finished the affidavit and the new set of probate papers and deposited them in his out box with a stenographic requisition slip.

When he left the office for the day, the streets were still wet from the thunderstorm, but the sky was blue and the air had a freshly-washed, sweet smell. Tim opted to walk home to his apartment, making his way over to Fifth Avenue and then up to Central Park. He cut across the park, where Frisbees were spinning, softball players were chattering encouragement to their teammates in languages he didn't always recognize, and a pair of lovers were lounging on the grass, oblivious to the dampness of the ground. Sabrett hot dog vendors hawked their wares alongside unlicensed entrepreneurs, whose jewelry, watches and other goods were rapidly folded up in their display cloths and trundled off to new business locations when a policeman moved too close. Happiness, New York City style, was in the air. The empty beer cans and other debris littering the greensward made it clear that this was not some bucolic setting in the Vermont countryside, even if one were not to look up at the apartments and hotels towering behind the tree line, but a certain tranquility and good feeling pervaded.

Tim reached his apartment building, in the Eighties on the West Side between Amsterdam and West End Avenues, an hour after he left the office. He climbed up the east stairway to the third floor, and walked down the hallway to the apartment he shared with his classmate.

The hallways, unlike the sidewalks, were still hot and stuffy. They smelled of dinners cooking and cooked, tonight's and perhaps yesterday's as well. Mrs. Marblestein, his neighbor from down the hall, bustled past him with her folding shopping cart, full of newly-purchased produce and the other ingredients of the evening meal.

"Your fresh roommate is back," she said.

"Rick? Rick's back?" asked Tim, surprised to hear that his roommate had bothered to return to the city so soon when he still didn't have a job. Tim quickly unlocked the door and went inside.

"Hey, Tim." Rick was sitting in the living room with a beer, watching the forlorn Mets play out their season on the black and white television, his bare feet propped sideways on the windowsill.

Uncharacteristically, he disengaged himself from this position and stood to greet Tim. "I tried to call you at the office but they said you'd left. That must've been an hour ago. I was starting to think the muggers finally took an interest in you, now that you're such a rich son of a bitch."

Tim laughed. "I didn't even get paid yet, Rick. Maybe that's why I got across the Park with my wallet intact. What brings you back so soon? Change your mind about hitchhiking around the country?"

"No way, my friend! That's still on," said Rick. "In fact, I've been through half of New England already. Picked up a ride from New London to Bridgeport yesterday, and as soon as I saw the billboard I knew I had to stop by to see your old man."

Suddenly Rick looked serious. Tim felt a cold chill grip his chest.

"Tim, your father. He had a stroke last night."

Tim paced, breathing heavily. "Oh, God. I just saw him last week."

"We were having a beer and talking about you, and all of a sudden what he was saying just didn't make sense, and then he passed out. I called an ambulance and they got him to the hospital. I think he's going to be okay, but they're keeping him for awhile."

"Do my sisters know?" Tim felt like he should sit down, but as soon as he found himself in a chair, he was up and pacing the room again.

"Yeah, Tim, and your older sister's husband, the one who's a doctor, he even examined your father himself when the ambulance got him to the hospital."

Tim stopped his pacing abruptly and looked at Rick.

"Why did you come down here? Why didn't you just call? Are you sure he's all right?"

"Oh, he is, don't worry. I would've called, but your father wanted me to contact somebody named Marge Conley first. And when I did, she told me not to call you. She didn't want you traveling up there alone, all upset and everything. So she sent me down to pick you up. Who is she, anyway?"

"She's just a girl I used to know," said Tim, feeling warmth where the chill had been before. "I ran into her up in Bridgeport after you and I took the bar exam, and we started going out."

15

BY THE TIME RICK DROPPED Tim at the hospital in Bridgeport, it was after 10 at night, and the lobby was deserted. Tim eventually found a receptionist on duty in the emergency room, and she was able to locate his father's data in her card index. Mr. O'Leary, she told him, was alive, and in the intensive care unit on the third floor, but inaccessible since visiting hours were over for the day. Tim went up anyway.

The first person he saw when he stepped out of the elevator was Marge. She hugged him.

"I think he's going to be okay, Tim, but they won't know everything until tomorrow at the earliest. He had some paralysis on one side at first, but that passed after a few hours."

They sat down on two chairs in the hallway.

"He still can't say much besides 'yep' and 'nope,' but the neurologist did some tests, and he said they were 'unremarkable,' to use his words. He said they didn't do an X-ray since X-rays don't work for the brain, because there's no 'contrast'—another one of his words. He also said some new device called a 'CAT scanner,' which would work, isn't available here yet. Anyway, he was pretty sure this was just a

'TIA'—sort of a small stroke. If it is, your dad could be talking and almost normal in a day or so."

"They said I couldn't see him, because visiting hours are over. Is that right?"

"Sure you can. I know the head nurse in ICU. Come on."

It didn't occur to him that there was anything unusual about Marge having this contact.

His father was out cold, and Tim might well have thought him dead, had he not been assured to the contrary by Marge, and satisfied in any event that the activity displayed on the various monitors around the bed proved that something was going on inside his father's body. He whispered a few words in the older man's ear, but received no response. He was about to sit down to begin his bedside vigil, when the toughest looking nurse he had ever seen hustled up to the foot of the bed.

"What are you two doing in here?" she hissed. "Don't you know visiting hours ended three hours ago?"

"This is my father, nurse. I just came up from New York when I heard what happened. Marge here knows the head nurse, and got her permission to bring me in."

"Well I'm the head nurse, sweetie." She eyeballed Marge. "If your friend knows me so well, she knows that I meant it an hour ago when I told her I'd call hospital security if I found her in here again after visiting hours. Now get out of here both of you, and don't come back." She escorted them out the door.

"You could have gotten us in trouble, Marge," complained Tim when they were alone again in the corridor.

"I don't think so, Tim. You don't have to spend much time being a private eye before you realize that it's almost impossible to get in trouble these days just for being where you're not wanted. Did you eat yet?"

"No, I came straight from my apartment with Rick, but I saw the hospital's cafeteria was closed before I came up here. I'm not going to break in to get something to eat, if that's what you have in mind."

"Don't be ridiculous Tim," she sighed. She stared at him intensely, unsure of herself in making her next suggestion, but determined not to let him descend into anxiety. "Let's go to Smokey's. Your father will probably sleep through the night now, anyway."

Tim nodded assent. Marge led him down a back stairway and out a side door, where they found Marge's car which, Tim noticed, was parked in the doctors' parking lot. Tim was starting to wonder about her.

The regulars looked up when Tim and Marge walked into Smokey's, but for once they left him alone. When one of them greeted him as "Tim" instead of "Heads," he knew they must have heard about his father. Even Toots was subdued when she took their drink orders. As she started to walk away, she turned and almost shyly asked Tim if his "Dad" was all right.

"I think so, Toots. We don't know for sure yet, but it looks like he may pull through."

"Blessed Mother of Mercy! That's good news, Tim. You know we're all pullin' for him here."

"I know you are, Toots. Thanks." Tim was back home.

He and Marge talked some more about his father, but after awhile there wasn't much left to say, so before long they were talking about his first few days at Bradford, Lord and Turner, and the Estate of Reginald V. Simpson. Marge was proud to hear that he was working on such a large estate, even though he told her it was only because all the experienced trusts and estates associates were away on vacation when Simpson died, and Rem Watson wanted to move quickly before Simpson's brother could think up a way to make trouble.

As she listened to his description of the last few day's events, she became fascinated with the part about the mysterious disappearance of the Simpson Will. Suddenly, interrupting his explanation of one of the tax questions he had been asked to research by another attorney at the firm, Marge cut in. "Tim, there's something wrong!"

The tension leapt back into Tim's face. "What is it? What didn't you tell me about Pop?"

"No, no. I'm sorry. I'm not talking about your father. It's Rex Simpson's Will. You said his new Will and his old Will were both signed out of the safe, but only the old one was signed back in."

"Right, but that was a mistake, because it was really the new one that was returned to the safe when the old one was removed to be destroyed."

"Either way, Tim, one of Simpson's Wills should be in the safe. Even Alice Tedesco said so. She saw an entry on the master list that indicated Rex Simpson's Will was in there. She saw that when she checked before the meeting, and she assumed it was the Will they were looking for, not realizing the entry referred to the previous Will. But neither Will is there. So someone stole it!"

"Stole it?" Tim was starting to wonder about Marge again. "It was just some partner who was too rushed or too cavalier about the rules to bother logging it out. It will probably turn up in someone's desk drawer next month, but by then the copy will have been probated, and I'll be researching a discovery motion for some litigation partner."

"Tim, don't be so naive. That guy Austin Chamberlain may have been dumb enough to get the new Will when he was supposed to fetch the old one, and then to sign the line next to the old one when he wanted to log the new one back in. But he's obviously too uptight about office rules to just forget about logging something in or out when he moves a Will. Alice Tedesco herself said Tom Quinn is too considerate of the staff to ignore office procedure, right? And it sounds like only a few of the partners do estate work. So what legitimate reason would the others have for removing Simpson's Will from the safe? The estate partners would have no reason to, unless they were working on Simpson's file, but it doesn't sound like any of them were. No, Tim, somebody took it on purpose and of course didn't log it out. Somebody stole it."

"Why, Marge? What would be the point? Especially when it's going to make the firm look bad, and all the partners would get hurt by that. No," he laughed. "You're not going to make this into more than it is. Not unless you can answer that question."

"Sorry, Tim, it's *you* who's going to have to answer that question."

— 16 —

TIM COMMUTED TO MANHATTAN from Bridgeport on Thursday and Friday, visiting his father first thing each morning, and again in the evening when he returned from work. His father's condition was steadily improving as one by one his faculties returned to normal, along with his idiosyncrasies. He told Tim Richard Nixon would make a good president but he wasn't so sure about Nixon's running mate "Spiral" Agnew. He didn't agree with the doctors who told him that he would have to stop smoking, since in his opinion smoking had a calming effect, which was just the opposite of the type of thing that led to strokes.

The Simpson case was basically on track, although the original Will was still missing. The alternate set of papers seeking probate of a "lost Will" had been finalized and signed, and Tim had been instructed to file them in the Manhattan Surrogate's Court on Monday morning. Given the delicacy of the situation, Austin Chamberlain would come along.

Marge Conway was still convinced that Rex Simpson's Will had not disappeared by accident. Tim's father, who was "virtually his old self" in the "comprehension department," according to the head nurse (who, Tim doubted, had ever met his father prior to this hospitalization), agreed with Marge and warned Tim to take her seriously.

On Friday evening, the doctors cleared Mr. O'Leary for transfer to a regular hospital room, and by Sunday it looked like Tim could stay at his apartment during the week, and keep in touch by phone.

The day before, Marge had suggested that Tim ought to start looking for a nicer apartment than his walk-up bachelor pad, as she referred to it, now that he was making a good salary. So after visiting Tim's father on Sunday morning, they picked up the New York Times and sat down together in the hospital's cafeteria. Scanning the real estate section for the Manhattan apartment listings, Marge circled a few as Tim browsed the sports section.

"Tim, there are at least a dozen in your price range that are within a mile or so of your office," she said, as Tim looked up. "And there are a bunch of open houses today. Let's drive into the city and take a look at a few. Then we could have dinner and I'll drive back to Connecticut after I drop you at your apartment. That way you won't have to take the train in the morning."

So off they went. The first open house was just off Third Avenue in the Seventies. It was listed as "full of light" with a "huge living room" and having "views of Midtown." Parking wasn't too bad, since it was a Sunday, and they walked the few blocks from the car to the apartment building.

"This is a nice neighborhood, Tim. I can't wait to see the apartment."

"Same here," said Tim. The area was indeed nice. The sidewalks were neatly swept, uniformed doormen stood under awnings at some of the building entrances, and flowers grew in the window boxes of the brownstones that shared the street with the apartment buildings.

Tim and Marge arrived at the address and went inside. The building had a small, but clean, lobby, and most importantly, an elevator. A broker's card taped to the wall next to the elevator announced the location of the open house as Apartment 3-G. They entered the elevator and headed up. This was exciting!

Apartment 3-G was down a short hallway to the right as they stepped out of the elevator. Its door was propped open slightly. Again, the broker had taped her card to the wall, and written "Come on in!" on it.

As they entered, the broker, a woman in her mid to late fifties, jumped up from the couch. Her smile was so radiant it warranted a cameo appearance on the "You'll wonder where the yellow went when you brush your teeth with Pepsodent" TV commercials.

"Hi! I'm Pearl, of Platinum Realty," she gushed as she came over, shaking hands with both of them. "Isn't this stunning? Just listed! You're lucky, it won't last."

"Hi, Pearl. I'm Tim O'Leary, and this is Marge Conley."

"Oh, perfect. Lovebirds! Oh, I'm so happy for you. Come and look around. Quick, before someone else comes in and snaps it up."

"Okay, Pearl. Could we see the living room first?"

"Why, you're standing in it, of course," she said, still beaming. "Isn't it great?"

"But the ad said it was 'huge.' I thought this was the foyer."

"Oh, you're funny, you are! Welcome to Manhattan. This is much bigger than most. Put a nice TV cabinet over there, then a love seat for the lovebirds and an easy chair for when you're alone, a coffee table and a lamp, wow. What else could anyone need?"

Tim started to wonder if Pearl ever ended a sentence with anything less than exuberance.

"Pearl, the ad said full of light, but it's a little dark in here."

"Oh, but Tim, you should see it in the morning. After all, today's a bit overcast, but on a sunny day it's spectacular.

Glass half full. Right, Marge?"

"Not sure when you were last outside, Pearl," said Marge. "It's a beautiful day. There's not a cloud in the sky."

"Well, in any case," interjected Tim, "where are the windows with the views of Midtown?"

"Oh, that's the showstopper all right," said Pearl, still smiling and waving them toward her. "Wait until you see the bedroom." She led them through a doorway.

"Voila!"

They entered the bedroom and stopped, because the near side of a bed, possibly a queen size but probably only a full, started just several inches past the open door. About eighteen inches past the bed on the far side was a small, curtained window. Marge made her way toward it to have a look at the view. There wasn't a lot of space between the foot of the bed and the wall to the right, but the room had no additional furnishings—not even a dresser—so Marge's path was unimpeded. Along the way, she stopped at what looked like a closet door and poked her head inside.

"This is the bathroom?" exclaimed Marge. "It's so small."

"So much the easier to clean, dear! So you have time for the more important things in life. You know," Pearl winked as she nodded toward the bed.

"But if this isn't a closet, where do you put your clothes?"

"Smart girl. Glad you asked. Why, right under the bed."

"You stick your clothes under the bed? Gross."

"No, silly. Look." Still smiling brightly. "There are drawers under the bed, and around the headboard, of course. Loads of space. And the bed comes with the apartment! So end of story, as far as drawer space is concerned."

Marge took a breath, decided to withhold further comment, and continued her short journey to the other side of the bed. Tim followed her. Together, they parted the curtains, looked out the window, and saw ...

"A brick wall?"

"Oh, no." Pearl waved her arms. "Turn your heads to the

left, you two."

Marge and Tim craned their necks to the left as instructed. At the end of a long corridor of brick, framed by the walls
of the apartment building and its neighbor six feet across the
way, they saw it. The top of a tree, a smaller building on the
far side of the street, and, just poking out above the water
tank atop a taller building further to the south, the very top
of the Empire State Building.

"Let's get out of here, Marge," whispered Tim. "I think
I'll stick with my place for now."

"Right, Tim. I'm with you. How do we escape without
offending Pearl?" she whispered.

"Let's try 'broker speak.'"

"Good idea."

"What are you two lovebirds whispering about now?"
Pearl chirped from the other side of the room.

"Spectacular!" said Tim.

"As advertised!" said Marge.

"Don't you just love it!" gushed Pearl.

"We'll get back to you, Pearl."

"Don't drag your feet! This one won't last!"

"We're on it, Pearl! Wonderful place! A winner, for sure.
Bye now, and all that good stuff!"

Pearl followed them to the door. "Call me."

"Will do."

Tim and Marge didn't wait for the elevator. Their "broker
speak" portfolio was exhausted, but they were afraid Pearl
had plenty left in the tank. They bolted for the fire exit, took
the stairs down and hurried out to the sidewalk.

"So much for apartment hunting, Marge."

"I'll drink to that, Tim. Let's go to dinner."

17

THE NEW YORK COUNTY SURROGATE'S COURT was located in the Hall of Records at 31 Chambers Street in Manhattan, just across from City Hall Park and catty-corner from the New York City Municipal Building. The Hall of Records was an old building, and once beautiful. Its exquisite exterior had gradually darkened from vehicle exhaust, and wear-and-tear and clutter from long-term municipal use cast a dull bureaucratic pallor over most of its otherwise dramatic interior.

Tim saw the building for the first time as he emerged from the IRT subway's Brooklyn Bridge station in the park across the street. His view was somewhat obstructed by an idling tour bus whose out-of-town passengers were gawking at an apparently illegally parked Volkswagen mini-van. It was covered with what Tim assumed were psychedelically inspired images of colorful scenes and images totally out of place in this grim environment.

Propped against the van's windshield, held in place by a broken windshield wiper, was a parking ticket. The dispenser of the ticket, a beleaguered New York City patrolman, seemed to be arguing with someone not yet visible to Tim.

As he crossed Chambers Street and stepped onto the sidewalk in front of the Hall of Records, he saw the rest of the spectacle that was riveting the tourists' attention. A dozen long-haired demonstrators, all of whom had apparently been squeezed into the Hippie Van, were chanting as they marched in ragged order. Carrying signs protesting the War in Vietnam, they shouted suggestions to "Make love, not war!" and loudly proclaimed, "Hell no, we won't go!"

As the policeman demanded that they move their vehicle, one of the hippies grabbed the parking ticket and returned it to him, along with a flower, an odd looking cigarette, and a suggestion that he "chill."

The cop was really getting pissed off now.

Someone pulled at Tim's sleeve. It was Austin Chamberlain.

"Are you all right, Tim? Let's get inside before this turns ugly. I'll never understand why they can't clean up the parts of this city that decent people have to use," he whined as he pulled Tim into the Hall of Records.

Tim wasn't so sure who "they" were, but he suspected that such a cadre of "Austin's Avengers" would not have stopped with the hippies if they were ever unleashed.

Once inside the building, the two of them took the elevator to the fifth floor and found the Surrogate's Court's Probate Department, a place Austin said he loathed visiting but "considering the gravity of the situation …"

Austin advised Tim that the primary job of a probate clerk in most metropolitan area counties was to discourage the probate of Wills, or at least to make the process as difficult and unpleasant as possible for a reputable attorney.

"It's just a shame, Tim. To give these creatures so much to say about something that really should be so routine. I mean, do they really think they have the right? You have no idea how demeaning it is to embark on a sophisticated piece of estate administration in this environment."

The crew in probate obviously had something to worry about once Austin's Avengers had finished up on the streets below.

Several attorneys were ahead of them, but they were finally seen by a middle-aged female clerk who, Tim had to admit, would not likely interview well for a job as a hospitality hostess at Disneyland.

"You can't file these here," were her first words, after she'd grumpily riffled through the Simpson probate papers for a few seconds.

"Where would you suggest we do put probate papers then, if not in the Probate Department?" replied Austin, in what may well have been an attempt at humor. Tim sensed the clerk might put a different spin on it.

"Have we made a mistake?" he interjected, with what he hoped was a sufficient degree of cowering humility to head off the clerk's likely response to Austin's request. It worked. The clerk, like a fighting bull focusing for a charge on the haughty toreador Austin, was diverted at the last moment by the inferior picador Tim. She turned toward him.

"You have to clear them with the Law Department on the fourth floor. It's a lost Will proceeding."

"Thanks," said Tim. He stood and gathered the papers before Austin had an opportunity to regain the clerk's attention.

"It's a good thing you intervened Tim, before I *just lost it* with that clerk," Austin huffed as they left the room. "Of all the bureaucratic nonsense. Well, at least the members of the law department have law degrees, although from what diploma mills I can't imagine."

Tim refrained from humming his alma mater's fight song on the way down to the fourth floor.

Two hours later, after several unexplained interruptions as the documents were passed from one person to another, and then back again, the law department had been relegated to Austin Chamberlain's doghouse along with the probate department and the cashier's office, but at last they were filed. Austin and Tim left the courthouse with a citation, issued by the Chief Clerk (a title of obviously questionable distinction, according to Austin), which directed Rex Simpson's brother Harold to "show cause" on August 29th, why the Will should not be probated by the Surrogate's Court. The timetable for service of the citation on Harold would be tight, but Rem had insisted that Harold be given "no time to breathe, much less to think, assuming he ever does."

"See our managing clerk about getting this citation out to a process server so it can be served on Harold Simpson, will you, Tim?" instructed Austin, hailing a taxi in front of the courthouse. "I've had about enough for today. I think I'll head back to civilization and take a few aspirin. See you tomorrow."

Tim watched Austin's cab pulling away from the curb, and then checked to see if the clash between the flower children and the constabulary might still be raging. It was not. The hippies and their van had moved on and the street was relatively quiet.

He headed for the subway, so he could return to the office and find out what a managing clerk was, not totally sure why Austin would have allowed anyone with the title of "clerk" to infiltrate his domain, but guessing (correctly, it turned out) that Austin did not mind clerks who did not think it their place to tell him what to do.

18

AUGUST 29TH WAS ONE of those beautiful late summer days in Manhattan, when the crowds have begun to thin out as the end of summer draws near, and anyone who can takes one last week in the Hamptons, or on the Jersey shore, or maybe in the mountains, before Labor Day ends it all for another year. A cool breeze had come down from the north and cleared the haze and the fumes from the air, which actually smelled fresh and clean that morning.

Tim was feeling upbeat as he crossed Chambers Street and climbed the few stairs to the entrance to the Hall of Records. Today he was to meet Austin in the hallway outside the senior Surrogate's courtroom on the fifth floor. In the world of a young "Wall Street Lawyer," this visit to a working courtroom represented something of an advance from his last trip to the courthouse three weeks earlier, when he had gotten only as far as the law department office.

In fact, if Tim had already been admitted to the bar, Chamberlain told him, he may well have been sent on his own to answer the call of the probate calendar that morning. Other, less reputable attorneys and firms might even send paralegals and secretaries to answer the calendar on uncontested probate matters, Austin said, but Bradford, Lord and Turner would never consider such unethical behavior. Tim's billing rate was much lower than his, of course, so had Tim been admitted Austin would have welcomed the chance to save the client some money by delegating this responsibility, seeing as how he "detested the sort of attorney who pads his bills by making these useless court appearances."

Tim made a mental note to check with Austin later about the ethics of billing the Simpson Estate for both of them being at court today.

Chamberlain was already standing outside the courtroom when Tim arrived. He stood out, Tim had to admit, with his impeccably-tailored summer-weight suit, properly-knotted conservative yet fashionable tie, highly-polished shoes, and Brooks Brothers button-down shirt. Other attorneys in the hall, dressed in more ordinary suits and ties, joked among themselves, pored over papers or huddled with their clients.

Austin saw him and called out as Tim approached.

"Tim, over here! That's my boy! What a day, what a glorious day! I've checked the calendar and we're right up there near the top. We should be out of here by ten, and I can be on my way to Quogue before noon. What a weekend it's going to be out there!" Austin was positively ecstatic. "Did you check with the office this morning?"

"Yes, I called from the pay phone in the hallway. The mail is in, and we've received nothing from Harold Simpson. No attorney's appearance, no objections, no nothing."

"Oh, that's great Tim, just great. Although, frankly I don't know why Rem is so concerned about Harold Simpson. Let's face it. Harold would never find a reputable firm willing to take on Bradford, Lord and Turner here. And even if he could, he certainly doesn't have the wherewithal to pay their fees. No. Rem's wrong on this one. Look around you, not a single attorney with the stature for the Simpson matter. And even if one were here, he wouldn't be representing Harold."

"Why not?" Tim was as always fascinated with Chamberlain's logic.

"Why? Because it would have been totally uncivil not to give me a call first."

Tim vowed to complain to one of his former professors about the dearth of adequate instruction in legal civility in the Fordham curriculum. It was obviously of similar significance as the first-name rule.

"Time to go in now, Tim. They should be calling the calendar in a few minutes." Austin pushed open the door, and they entered the courtroom.

The Manhattan Surrogate's Court or, more properly, the New York County Surrogate's Court, had two judges, while all of the other counties had only one. In some rural counties, the judge of the surrogate's court had to do double duty as a judge of one of the other state courts as well. There was talk from time to time of Kings County, more commonly known as Brooklyn, getting a second surrogate. Whether this was to compensate it for the loss a decade earlier of its beloved Brooklyn Dodgers, or for some other reason, was unclear, but the rumors persisted. For the moment, at least, Manhattan reigned supreme and, as befits the richest borough in the richest city on earth, its Surrogate's Court was also endowed with two of the most stunning courtrooms in the state.

They were elaborately paneled and fitted with benches, chairs and tables for attorneys, court clerks and law department personnel, and for jurors and the occasional member of the public who might wish to exercise his or her constitutional right to observe the dispensation of justice.

The courtroom in which Tim found himself this morning was not so much deep as it was wide, with intricately carved dark paneling, red carpeting, a two-story-high ceiling and an upper gallery, the use of which was reputedly once reserved for female spectators. One wit had later commented that the opening of the legal profession to women did not constitute an "elevation" in their status, but instead a demotion, altitude-wise.

Tim was awestruck. He felt himself warming to what he suspected was Austin Chamberlain's view of the practice of law—a courtly rivalry, pursued in subdued tones by a civilized few, who recognized the excellence of their peers and engaged in stimulating intellectual debate over interesting points of law involving large sums of money. He settled into the seat next to the one Chamberlain now occupied, and absorbed his surroundings with a pleasant detachment.

Even the lawyers, speaking quietly now or simply reading court papers in their seats, added to the majesty of the setting. After all, thought Tim, how often can one see a crowded space in New York City where not one person is shabbily dressed or apparently on the verge of committing an antisocial act?

At precisely 9:50 a.m.—20 minutes behind schedule—the judge, a man in his early sixties, took the bench and instructed his court attendant to call the calendar. Grouped according to categories, the matters on the calendar started with the probate proceedings requiring some action that day. Most of them, the Simpson Estate included, were on the calendar because those persons entitled to contest probate, usually close relatives, had been served with a citation. The citation ordered them to advise the court on this day if they had any objection to the validity of the Will.

Tim watched the action unfold as each case was addressed. When the court attendant called out the decedent's name, the estate attorney would rise to his feet, announcing that he was "for the petitioner" or, more commonly, "for the decree." Most of the Wills were unopposed, and those files were simply marked with directions for the clerks to prepare a probate decree for the judge to sign. Occasionally, however, an attorney other than the estate attorney, or an unrepresented person who had been served with a citation, would also stand. After identifying themselves, all would be told to "approach the bench," so they could discuss the matter with the judge. When an attorney was accompanied by his client, Tim noticed, there tended to be a bit of posturing on the attorney's part. In the end, though, the judge always seemed to schedule either a conference, or a date for the taking of testimony from the witnesses to the Will, or a deadline for the unrepresented to get themselves an attorney. Animated as the attorneys might become in describing their cases to the judge, it was quickly obvious that none were going to be won or lost today.

The calendar call progressed swiftly, but every time a group approached the bench, Chamberlain frowned and glanced at his watch. He was clearly anxious to catch the early train to Quogue for the start of the Labor Day weekend.

After fifteen minutes, at 10:05, the court attendant bellowed "Reginald V. Simpson."

Austin was on his feet at once. Before Tim could join him, he had already begun to speak, in the clipped, nasal tones which were so common in the corridors of Bradford, Lord and Turner, but decidedly less so in other parts of the city, even in rather dignified public settings such as this courtroom. Several heads turned, and their faces were not hostile—after all, every one of them would have liked to handle an estate, even if only just one time, as substantial and lucrative as the kind which must have lured this fellow into their midst. For once, Tim enjoyed being seen with Austin.

"Austin Chamberlain, your honor, of Bradford, Lord and Turner, for the petitioner Morgan Guaranty Trust Company." Tim realized Austin had rehearsed this, probably relishing the attention he was receiving from his less fortunate peers. He did, however, finish with the more pedestrian "For the decree."

"Not so fast!"

The faces which had turned toward Chamberlain while he spoke now pivoted at once toward the rear of the courtroom, most with mouths dropping slightly open, more startled than horrified. It was like someone had opened the courtroom door and let in a belligerent vagrant who had come up from the city streets five stories below.

Chamberlain, apparently assuming that this outburst could in no way relate to him, composed himself and repeated, "For the decree, your honor." Perhaps he hoped the surrogate would send the Simpson file on for processing before attending to this disturbance.

"I said, Not ... So ... Fast!"

This time Austin turned, as did Tim. Standing directly behind them, three rows back, was Michael Finley. Next to Finley stood a man with a leering boozer's face. A man Tim knew had to be Harold Simpson.

19

"WHO THE HELL is Mickey Finn?"

The question came from Rem Watson. Chamberlain and Tim were in his office, where they had gone straight from the courthouse. Austin was so shaken by the time he left the courtroom that he hadn't thought to call ahead, so Watson's secretary, Virginia Martin, had to go looking for Rem while Austin and Tim waited in his office. While she did, Austin called his wife to tell her to cancel their dinner reservations at the Westhampton Country Club. He was totally demoralized, and angry to boot. He'd provided Virginia with no explanation of the need for an immediate conference with Rem, other than instructing her to "Tell him Harold Simpson has hired some cretin who goes by the name Mickey Finn."

Watson's opening question on returning to the office indicated that this had not been enough. Austin elaborated.

"He's a Court Street lawyer, Rem. Torts, criminal, divorce, whatever he can lay his hands on."

"And his name is Mickey Finn? That's not a real name. It's something a crooked bartender slips into your drink so he can rob you."

"Well he said that's what I should call him. His real name is Finley. That's what he told the judge when we were asked to give our appearances. 'Michael Moriarity Macauley Finley,' he said. The court reporter asked if that was the name of his firm or just his name, and he said 'both.' Trying to be funny, I suppose."

"All right. I guess this is something we'll have to deal with. Was Harold with him?"

"Yes he was, Rem. They were both in court this morning. I haven't had the misfortune to meet the man before today, but from anything I've heard this was typical Harold—insufferable. He just stood there smirking, loving the whole thing. And Finley. He's obnoxious, offensive, disgusting. Not an iota of professional courtesy in him. He delights in amusing the audience, no matter what embarrassment he might cause a fellow attorney. I believe the firm would be fully justified in filing a grievance against him. Why he hasn't been disbarred is a total mystery to me! After all—"

"Is Harold contesting probate?" interrupted Rem, with a hint of impatience in his voice.

"Well, I can't imagine how he could, Rem. We were just as careful about the execution of Rex Simpson's Will as we always are. All of our procedures were followed to the letter."

"All except the one about not losing the Will." Watson's annoyance was now more patent, and Tim began to feel uncomfortable.

"Now that's unfair, Rem. That was just an administrative snafu. No surrogate is going to allow a person like Harold to break Rex Simpson's Will because of something like that." Chamberlain sniffed.

"Don't juries decide probate contests, Austin?" Rem was not even pretending to respect Chamberlain's opinion now. Tim thought it best that he leave the room. He started to rise from his chair.

Too late.

"Tim, I'd like to hear your observations," said Rem.

"What did you see in court today?"

Tim sat down. He said nothing. Could think of nothing.

"Tim?"

"Yes, Rem?"

"You did go to court with Austin this morning, didn't you?"

"Yes, Rem." Tim knew he should have something to offer now, but he had thought Austin sounded good, yet had obviously failed his screen test. His mind raced, but with no greater effect on his ability to vocalize than a good engine has on a car's ability to move when its transmission is shot.

"Tim, just tell me who said what to whom, and when. Start with your meeting up with Finley."

Tim found his voice. "We didn't meet with Finley, Rem, we just heard him."

"When was that?"

"It was in the courtroom. They had just called our case. Austin stood up to tell the surrogate that this firm was representing the bank, and that we would like the Will probated. Then someone yelled 'Not so fast' from behind us. I turned around and saw it was Mr. Finley."

"How did you know who he was?" Watson seemed surprised that Tim could identify a person like Finley. So did Chamberlain, who had been sulking in his chair since his diatribe against Finley had been interrupted.

"He offered me a job."

"Today?" Watson was appalled.

Austin appeared not to be. He rolled his eyes and shook his head, sighing as he said, "This is the kind of man we're dealing with, Rem. I told you Finley was a disgusting individual."

"Oh, no," Tim blurted. "I'm sorry. He didn't offer me a job today. That was months ago. I turned him down when your offer came through."

Watson seemed relieved. Chamberlain disappointed.

"All right, Tim. What happened then?"

"After he offered me the job?"

"Tim, I'm trying to find out what happened in court today." Watson looked like he was about ready to throw both of these boobs out.

Tim reddened. "Sorry, Rem. I should have realized that. I just got confused."

"Don't worry about it. Just go on, please."

"When I turned around and saw Mr. Finley, he was standing up, looking angry. Another man was standing next to him, sort of smirking, like Austin said. The other people in the courtroom seemed to recognize Mr. Finley also. Some of them looked surprised that he had shouted, but others were smiling."

"Why were they smiling?"

"I think they thought it was fun to watch him in action."

"You said Mr. Finley looked angry. Do you think he was?"

"I did then, but now I don't know."

"What changed your opinion?"

"He really did look angry, Rem, and he sounded angry." Tim was starting to feel better, now that he realized that all Watson wanted was a reasonably reliable eyewitness account of the morning's events. "But when the judge was finished with our case and went on to the next one, Mr. Finley turned around and gave me a smile and a wink before he left the courtroom. He said, 'This is fun, ain't it, kid?'"

"I see. I think that tells us something about Finley, don't you, Tim? He's obviously one of those attorneys who enjoys his courtroom theatrics, but who doesn't thrive on across-the-board meanness, like some of the 'take no prisoners' types we run into from time to time. So he's able to ingratiate himself with some of the people he wants to ingratiate himself with. He'll probably stick to these tactics as long as he thinks he can get our goat." Watson glanced at Chamberlain, who winced. Then he turned back to Tim.

"What happened after Finley yelled, 'Not so fast'?"

"Well, Austin didn't realize whoever had said that was

talking to us, so he asked the judge again for a probate decree."

"And what did the judge say to that?"

"He didn't have a chance to say anything, because Mr. Finley yelled 'Not so fast' again, even louder this time, and slower. And then the judge told us to all come up to the front so he could talk it over with us."

"He asked you to approach the bench?"

"Yes." Tim realized that Watson would appreciate hearing a few legal terms now and then in his high priced young associates' eyewitness accounts. He resolved to try incorporating some. "Yes Rem, and we did. When we were all before the judge, he asked us to tell the court reporter who we were and why we were there."

Tim noticed a bemused lift of Watson's eyebrow, and he rephrased his last answer. "You know. We gave the court reporter our appearances. When that was done, the judge asked Finley if he wanted to examine the attesting witnesses and the attorney who prepared the Will. He said he certainly did, and then he told the judge that both Austin and this firm should be investigated for our 'blatant attempt to mislead the court into probating a Will that doesn't even exist' and our 'scurrilous attempt to deprive Harold Simpson of his rightful inheritance in order to reap unconscionable fees from the greedy co-conspirator.' I think he meant the bank."

Chamberlain rejoined the conversation. "Can you believe this, Rem? The man's conduct was outrageous. It was slander of the worst sort."

Watson cut him short. "Go on, Tim."

Austin stewed.

"Well, the judge said okay to the first part and just sort of ignored the second," Tim went on. "The attesting witnesses and the attorney-draftsman are to appear in the Surrogate's Court on October fifteenth to testify. Since Austin drafted the Will, he will have to testify, and you and your secretary will also have to testify, since the two of you acted as witnesses to the Will signing."

"Makes sense," said Rem, nodding. Austin looked away as Tim continued.

"Then after the examinations are finished, Harold Simpson has ten days to decide whether or not he will object to probate. When he heard that, Mickey Finn said—I'm sorry, I shouldn't be calling him that, I guess."

"Makes no difference, Tim," said Rem. "Sounds like the name suits him. Go ahead."

"Okay. He said, 'We don't need ten days, judge. We don't need ten minutes. We're ready to file our objections right now, your honor. Mr. Chamberlain here is about to learn that the law does not look kindly on those who help themselves to the funds of widows and orphans.'"

"Widows and orphans? Who was he talking about?"

"I don't know, Rem."

"What did the judge say?"

"He seemed to be enjoying listening to Mr. Finley, at least for a while, so he didn't say anything at first. But he finally stopped him and said 'Mr. Finley, you can file your client's objections any time you want. All you need is a check for the filing fee.' Then Mickey Finn said, 'Our objections are burning a hole in my pocket, your honor. But I will just have to hold onto them until then, in deference to my poor client's reduced financial straits, considering the filing fee you have so kindly brought to my attention.'"

"How much is this filing fee, Tim?"

"Twenty-five dollars if he demands a jury trial. Otherwise, it's fifteen dollars." Tim was pleased to finally have an answer to a legal question, even one as mundane as this, at his fingertips. It just so happened that Tom Quinn had mentioned it when Tim had asked for a briefing on probate procedure the week before.

"Twenty-five dollars? You mean Finley is worried about Harold Simpson coming up with chickenfeed like that? How in the world is Finley being paid? He must figure there's enough money here that we'll lay something on the table to get rid of Harold and he can make a quick score."

"Will we, Rem?" Tim hadn't thought about the case being settled.

"We may just have to, Tim, if that missing Will doesn't show up soon. In the meantime, though, I want you to help me prepare for those examinations. And I want you to get the beneficiary in here so we can brief him on the status of the case. We may as well break the settlement idea to him at the same time. And he'll need counsel. Austin, you won't mind if I take the wheel from here on, will you?"

Austin didn't mind.

20

FINLEY DEMANDED that Rem leave the room.

It was October fifteenth, and Watson, Tim, Austin, Virginia Martin and Greg Trout were sitting across from Finley and Harold Simpson at a worn wooden table in a small room in the courthouse. A court reporter with a transcribing machine sat at the end of the table, busily taking down everything said by those present. Although in the same building, the room bore no resemblance to the grandeur of the Surrogate's courtroom. It was a place where some of the more mundane business of the court was conducted—in this case the examination under oath of the attorney who drafted Rex Simpson's Will and the people who watched him sign it. The tension, which Tim could feel the moment the combatants assembled, rose exponentially at this apparently unexpected request by opposing counsel.

"What are you talking about, Michael?" said Rem, somehow already on a first name basis with Finley, much to Tim's surprise.

"You're a witness, Watson. You witnessed the signing of the Will and I'm going to examine you today. So you can't stay in the room while I examine the other witness and the lawyer who drafted the Will, this Chamberlain fellow here. Those are the rules. Actually, now that I think of it, he's got to leave, too, because I'm going to examine Miss Martin here first."

Finley apparently preferred last names to first as a familiar form of address, but Tim suspected this was not designed to make an adversary comfortable.

"What rules are you talking about?" Rem asked, seeming more bemused than annoyed by Finley's opening gambit.

Finley chortled. "You guys know as well as I do that I can ask a witness to leave the room when another one is testifying. You two will just have to go."

"But that doesn't apply here, Michael. We're present in our capacity as attorneys for the petitioner, Morgan Guaranty. We're not just witnesses," Rem replied. "The court is not going to allow you to conduct these examinations while one party is unrepresented."

"What do you mean unrepresented, Watson? The kid doesn't have to leave."

With a sudden feeling of dread, Tim realized that he was the "kid."

"The kid, as you refer to him, is not even admitted to the bar yet. He's here to observe and learn. He can't represent anybody," Rem replied, still quite composed. Austin, in contrast, fidgeted and squirmed. He clearly recoiled at the thought of having to submit to questioning by this offensive representative of those he considered to be the malignant underside of what he believed should be a noble, and exclusive, profession.

"Suit yourself, Watson. But either you two leave or I do. Rules are rules, and if you want to wait until the kid gets his license before we get going, it's just fine with me. But don't forget to tell Mr. JP Morgan here that we expect him to keep a good eye on my client's money while we're waiting for you."

"I think we'd better get a ruling on this, *Mister* Finley," Rem sighed, apparently no longer on a first name basis with Mickey Finn. "Let's see if we can find someone in the law department."

The lawyers, the court reporter, and the not-quite-yet-admitted-to-practice lawyer Tim rose from the table and headed to the law department to see whose position would be vindicated in this preliminary skirmish. Greg Trout a/k/a Mr. JP Morgan was told to stay behind, as were Virginia Martin and Harold Simpson, who was studying the Daily Racing Form.

Walking through the hallway, while Chamberlain remonstrated with Watson about the deplorable lack of civility displayed by their adversary, Finley pulled Tim aside. "Remember that intern I told you about, kid?" he murmured in Tim's ear, as they strolled behind the others. "He's the one who came up with this idea. I guess these big shot Ivies didn't have it in their script for today."

"But, Mr. Finley, do you really think the court will make them stay out of the room? I mean, Mr. Watson is the lawyer."

"Nah, kid, they'll let him stay."

"Then why did you do it?"

"Always keep them off balance, kid. Don't let them get comfortable. They've got problems here and they know it, or at least Watson does. That nitwit Chamberlain thinks we should all wear powdered wigs, call the judge 'Your Grace,' and hold our conferences at some Hamptons country club."

They arrived at their destination. A woman was sitting at a desk with a name plate reading "Elizabeth Marks, Law Department Secretary."

"Here we are!" bellowed Finley. "What do you say, Betty?"

"I say we should start patrolling the river crossings," she said with a smirk, "to keep scoundrels like you from coming over into Manhattan. First time I've seen you since they transferred me from Kings Supreme. What are you doing here, anyway? I didn't know we had any small claims cases on the calendar today."

"Simpson, Betty. Like in probate proceedings—my specialty."

Watson raised an eyebrow, while Chamberlain muttered something inaudible.

"Simpson? You're running in some fast company, Mickey. Better be careful."

"Don't worry about me, Betty. These gentlemen and I need a ruling. Who do we see?"

She checked her calendar.

"Jack Zaggert is handling rulings today. Go on in and see him. I'll let him know you're coming. Don't give him any grief, Mickey, or you'll have to answer to me."

"Don't you worry, dear. I'll be my usual polite and considerate self. You know me."

"I certainly do, Mickey. I certainly do."

21

THREE DAYS LATER, Austin, Tim and Rem emerged from the building, the examinations at an end but the final outcome very much in doubt. Jack Zaggert, the law department attorney assigned to their case, had suggested that Mickey Finn's demand was "a bit over the top." He acknowledged a rule allowing attorneys to insist that witnesses not be present while others were testifying, lest they tailor their own testimony to make it consistent with the others'. He believed there must be an exception, however, for an attorney actually involved in the case who happened to be a witness as well. At the same time, he warned, if the attorney (Rem Watson in this case) was to be called to testify at trial, it might be necessary for him to step aside and allow an unaffiliated attorney to actually try the case. For now, he suggested a compromise that satisfied everyone. Rem was to go first, with neither Austin nor Virginia in the room. He would then remain, in his capacity as Morgan Guaranty's attorney, while Virginia was examined. Austin could not be there for Virginia's testimony, though, since he was also a witness and would not have testified yet, unless Finley was willing to examine him out of order, which he was not. Tim could attend to take notes and otherwise help Watson. Everyone agreed that Austin could leave, and then return the next morning for his own examination.

This suited him just fine, especially since, as he privately informed Rem Watson, he was on the verge of an emotional meltdown from having to tolerate what he referred to as "the nauseatingly boorish behavior of that cretin Finley and his lowlife client," and that he planned to call his doctor immediately so that a prescription for valium or some other calming medication could be written and filled before the day was over.

Austin departed for the office. Watson and Martin were then deposed. Both testified that they had witnessed the signing of the Will, and that Rex had gone out of his way to make it very clear that he wanted his brother Harold to receive absolutely nothing from his estate. This was not a surprise to Finley, who already knew that if the Will still existed, it would be found to be valid. He had gotten to know his client well enough to have no illusions about whether the Will did or did not truly represent Rex's wishes with respect to his brother. He did, however, gain some satisfaction from the inability of Virginia Martin to be absolutely certain that it was the earlier Will she had put into the envelope with the letter sent to Rex Simpson. She had to admit that both Wills were originals and would have looked very similar to one another, except of course if she were to have checked the date on the signature page, which she could not say for sure she had.

The relative calm that pervaded the first day's examinations did not continue into the second day, when Chamberlain came back to take the hot seat. Within minutes, Finley asked him if he was being treated for mental illness after Austin had to admit, upon being asked a "throwaway" question about whether he was taking any medications, that he had taken valium before his examination that morning.

Finley knew that this was the person who had signed the Will out from Bradford, Lord and Turner's Will safe and nev-

er signed it back in. So for an excruciating—to Austin, anyway—two days, Finley hammered him with an endless series
of painful questions the likes of which, in Austin's mind at
least, would have tested the bounds of propriety even if addressed to a disgraced attorney facing disbarment. A sample
exchange between Finley and Austin went like this:

"How many other Wills has your firm lost?"

"Not one."

"Until now?"

"We still haven't."

"So you put Mr. Simpson's old Will back in the safe?"

"No, I put the new one in."

"But it's not there."

"No."

"The log book says you put the old one in."

"Yes, but that was a mistake."

"How do you know that?

"Because I remember."

"Well, do you remember taking two Wills out?"

"Two Wills?"

"Yes, the log book says you took out the new Will and
then the old Will."

"Right, first the new one and then the old one."

"And you put the old one back."

"No, I put the new one back."

"So where is the new one?"

"That's what I can't figure out."

"And where is the old one?"

"I think that went to Mr. Simpson."

"But you don't know?"

"Well, Rem says he sent it to Mr. Simpson."

"Did Rem put it in the envelope?"

"Oh, certainly not. Secretaries do that."

"So he doesn't know, either?"

"Well, Virginia would have made sure she put the Will in
the envelope before sending out the letter."

"She got the old Will from you?"

"Well, yes."

"But you had put the old Will back in the safe?"

"Well, not really."

"Not really?"

"No, that was a mistake, like I said before."

"All right, let me get this straight. You say first you took the new Will out of the safe by mistake, right?"

"Right."

"And when you realized your mistake, you put it back, right?"

"Right."

"And took the old one out?"

"Right."

"And wrote down in the log book that you had now taken that one out?"

"Yes."

"And wrote down that you had put it right back in, but that was another mistake, since what you really meant was that it was the new one that you put back in?"

"Right. Now you've got it."

"So, where is the new one?"

"I told you I don't know."

"But it's certainly not in the safe where you said you put it, right?

"Right."

"Didn't it wind up going to Mr. Simpson with the other one in that envelope?"

"Well, I certainly hope not."

"Has your staff scoured every inch of your safe for that Will?"

"Yes, we had that done the minute we learned the Will was missing."

"And were other areas searched as well?"

"Absolutely. We take our clients' interests very seriously. We basically had every person in the office search every file, every desk drawer, every briefcase, every nook and cranny of the office for that Will. We brought all of our rather considerable resources to bear on the problem," lamented Chamberlain, "but to no avail."

"And the new Will has not been found among the late Mr. Simpson's effects?"

"No, not there either."

"Nor has the old one?"

"No."

"So he destroyed them both?"

"I didn't say that."

"You didn't have to."

And this was the gentle part. After two days Finley announced that he was finished with Mr. Chamberlain, and that he would file his client's objections and a jury demand in the morning. It was obvious, he said, that the last Will was sent to the late Mr. Simpson with Watson's letter. Clearly, Mr. Simpson had destroyed it when he realized the great injustice he had done to his only living relative, his dear brother Harold. The new Will should thus be denied probate without further ado, before this travesty of justice be permitted to proceed any further.

As soon as they were outside, Austin announced his intention of going straight home to recuperate from his mistreatment at the hands of "that dreadful man." Rem bade him a speedy recovery, and headed toward the subway with Tim. As they crossed the street, Tim asked Rem a question which had been puzzling him since the day Michael Finley appeared in court and announced his intention to object to probate.

"Harold gets nothing under any of Mr. Simpson's old Wills. I saw them in the file that the firm kept for Rex and his wife before their divorce. What's the point of breaking this one if Harold just loses out in the end, anyway?"

"That's why Finley didn't try to hurt me or Virginia during our examination, Tim," Rem sighed. "If the new Will was valid when signed, it revoked all of Rex's prior Wills. Revoking the new one later on doesn't revive the old ones—they're still dead. Harold is Rex's sole distributee—his next of kin. He takes the whole estate if this one goes down."

22

LATER THAT FALL, Tim stood outside the New York Times office in Times Square, where its central printing press was located, nervously waiting for the first edition of the day's newspaper to emerge. It would contain the results of July's bar examination. Many others stood shivering on the dark sidewalk with him. Finally, several bales of the paper were tossed unceremoniously out the door to the street vendors, who could barely cut the stout twine holding the bales together before hundreds of hands thrust money at them and grabbed for the papers. Tim's hands were among them.

He passed.

Most of the others did as well, but some did not, and the extremes of joy and despair were evident to the puzzled passersby. Tim raced for a pay phone and called Marge.

"Congratulations, Tim! Oh, I knew you could do it. How should we celebrate?"

"How about coming down to Manhattan on Friday? We can spend the weekend in New York. I think Mayor Lindsay promised not to cause any more strikes until the election is over."

They decided to start in Little Italy in lower Manhattan. Never having been, Tim looked forward to it, excited to experience a taste of authentic Italian atmosphere and cuisine. Maybe they might even see one of those processions where the locals marched down the main street carrying a litter holding a seated, flower-bedecked Madonna. It would of course be followed by a priest sprinkling holy water over the crowds lining the procession route, and altar boys carrying lighted candles and swinging incense burners emitting fragrant clouds of scented smoke.

Tim met Marge's train at Grand Central Terminal on Friday evening. After a quick hug and a kiss, they hurried down to the subway and boarded the downtown Lex. Fifteen minutes later, they stepped out of the train at Canal Street and went quickly up the stairs, their excitement mounting with each step. Once on the sidewalk, they headed east.

After a block or two, Marge looked around. "Tim, are you sure we got off at the right stop? I don't think we're in Little Italy. I think we're in Chinatown." The crowds they were threading their way through had a distinctly Asian appearance.

"Mulberry Street is a few blocks further, Marge. We must just be in the outer fringes of Chinatown. I think this'll change in a minute."

They quickened their step, but their pace was slowed by masses of pedestrians clogging the narrow sidewalks. Many of them spilled over into the not much wider streets and vied with the barely moving vehicles for a place on the roadway. All moved in different directions, making progress even more difficult, but Tim and Marge finally reached Mulberry Street and saw what looked like restaurants with Italian names to their left, so they headed that way. These were the first ones they had seen in their three block walk that displayed signs written in an alphabet with which they were familiar. No featherless fowl hung beak down in the windows. They had arrived in Little Italy.

"This must be where it starts, Marge."

"Thank goodness. Still, I don't see any dangerous characters in trench coats, snap brim hats and dark glasses smoking cigarettes and looking for trouble."

"I think that's a movie stereotype. They don't do much of that stuff anymore, assuming they ever did."

"I know, Tim. Just kidding. Let's pick one of these restaurants and have dinner."

As she said it, Marge was immediately accosted by a man standing outside one of the restaurants which lined both sides of the street.

"This is the place, young lady. Buona sera to you and the young man. There is no finer Italian food anywhere on this side of the Atlantic! The pasta! It will melt in your mouth. Antipasti? Say no more! Bruschetta, prosciutto e melone, then pasta e fagioli! Calamari, osso bucco! Like my sweet mother used to make. Mamma mia. Oh, it brings tears to my eyes. And the wines! Chianti, Soave, Montepulciano, Orvieto, it goes on and on. We have it all, and the perfect atmosphere for you to enjoy it. At reasonable prices. Come in. Avanti! We will treat you like family."

He turned around to reach for the door so he could show them in, and, pointing toward the restaurant window, he excitedly exclaimed, "My goodness! This is your lucky day. The couple sitting at our best table, the one right by the window—they are just about to get up. It's almost as if they knew you were coming. Perfetto!"

Reeling from the verbal barrage, Tim started toward the door immediately, but Marge held him back.

"It does look nice, Tim, but maybe we should walk around and check out some of the others first. We can always come back."

"Good idea. We've got plenty of time."

Tim thanked the man and said they would probably be back.

"The table may not still be available, sir," was the fellow's dour reply, now with a look of concern on his face.

Marge assured him that they would not wander far, and they headed on up the street. 50 feet further on, they were again greeted by a stranger, this time a woman standing in front of another restaurant. She smiled and called out to them.

"You made the right choice, you two. This is the place with the best fare on the street, bar none. And we're rated three stars by the food editor of Il Progresso. I won't mention any names, but I can't say the same for some of the other places around here." She rolled her eyes left, toward the gentleman they had just met, who was oblivious to her indictment, having already turned his attention to an elderly couple. They seemed interested in the table by the window to which he was pointing.

"Thanks, but we're just out for a stroll," lied Marge. "Your restaurant does look nice, though. Maybe we'll be back later."

As they walked along, they received no fewer than a dozen such invitations.

"I think I get the picture," said Tim. "We'd better make a decision before one of them says he works for Carlo Gambino and his boss would not be pleased if we showed disrespect for his establishment."

"Okay, you're probably right. How do you propose we decide?"

"How about we flip a coin? Heads we stay on this side of the street. Tails we cross to the other side. Then flip it again—heads we go left, tails we go right. Then we walk one hundred steps and stop. Whatever restaurant we're standing in front of then is the one where we have dinner."

"You're weird, Tim. I never noticed that before. You just thought this up?"

"No. I read it in a book somewhere, but it seems like a good idea. Got any others?"

"No, let's go with it. I'm getting hungry."

The first coin flip resulted in their crossing the street. The second made them turn right. The 100 steps brought them across Hester Street and ended as they stood in front of a Chinese restaurant.

"Good grief, Tim. I think we'd better go back to the first place and see if the table by the window is still available. Maybe they got four stars in Il Progresso."

"Deal."

As they approached the restaurant, they saw that the table by the window was unoccupied and they quickened their pace. The gentleman at the door welcomed them back and complimented them on their decision to return. He led them toward the rear of the restaurant.

"But we thought the table by the window was available," Tim protested.

"Oh yes, that one. Very nice, but it's a little drafty up there, and I'm afraid there *is* some traffic noise that comes through those old windows. I'll get you a nice cozy table back here. Much better, much better. I see now you are not our typical tourists. You are a man of respect, a man who carefully considers his decisions. You and the lady should not be on display for every passing tourist to ogle. You are entitled to your privacy."

Just then Tim noticed the elderly couple he had seen out on the street an hour before. The gentleman, who was sitting with his wife at one of the "cozy" tables in the back of the restaurant, was asking the people at the next table if they minded getting up for a second so he could get by, apparently to make a trip to the men's room. They complied with his request, but only after asking *their* neighbors to do the same so that they could step into the narrow aisle between the rows of tables and a path could be cleared for the gentleman to extricate himself.

Tim tapped their host on the shoulder. "I think we'd prefer to sit at the table by the window, drafts and street noise notwithstanding."

"Oh, I'm sorry sir. I just remembered. We do have a reservation for that table in just a few minutes. I think you'll be perfectly happy right here. It's very private." He began to place menus on a small table next to a door which suddenly opened as a waiter rushed through with several plates of what appeared to be steaming mounds of pasta. The door banged against the "very private" table.

Tim and Marge looked at one another.

"Three stars?"

"Three stars."

They turned and fled the restaurant before the host could protest, racing next door and diving past the lady and into her restaurant before she could even assure them they had made the right decision. She grabbed two menus and showed them to a small but accessible table in the middle of the restaurant.

"Can I get you something to drink while you look at the menu?" she inquired.

"Yes, you can, Miss. Marge, how about a bottle of Chianti so we can start to get back to feeling like we thought we would when we came down here?"

"Sounds good to me, Tim."

"Okay! One bottle and two glasses, Miss."

"Very good, sir. I'll be back in a minute with the wine."

A half hour and several glasses of wine later, Tim and Marge were feeling much more mellow. They finished their appetizers and listened to the piped-in music which, although not live and a little heavy on the sentimental, was getting them into a dreamy, almost like being in Italy, mood. Just then, they were treated to an unexpected surprise—live music. A small bald mustachioed musician playing an accordion and singing Italian melodies entered the restaurant.

"Oh, Tim, this is great. Let's ask him to sing 'Volare.' It's my favorite."

"Hey, amico, per favore." Tim hoped his pronunciation wasn't too bad. He also hoped the man spoke English. He had just used up most of his Italian vocabulary.

The singer raised a bushy eyebrow and came over to their table.

"You speak Italian, mister?"

"No, that's about it. I wasn't sure you'd even understand that much. My pronunciation isn't that good. Please don't be offended by the way I mangled your language. You being Italian and everything."

"I'm not Italian."

"Oh, no offense. I know you're American now, and we're glad to have you. What part of Italy were your relatives from?"

"They're not from Italy. I'm Russian," he grinned. "Russkie. You want me to sing something for you and your lady?"

Marge giggled. "How about 'Volare,' comrade?"

"Sure, I know that one, my krasavitsa," he said, kissing her hand.

"What does that word mean?" asked Tim, hoping he wouldn't have to stand up to defend Marge's honor.

"It means beautiful woman, my lucky friend," said the Russian.

Marge giggled again, and Tim took her hand from across the table as the man launched into a workmanlike, if somewhat raucous version of the Italian classic. When he finished, Tim handed him a dollar bill and watched him move away, looking for other prospects. Before long, he headed off to serenade the patrons of the next restaurant.

Tim turned to Marge.

"Maybe Little Italy isn't what it used to be."

"Well at least there were no gangsters shooting at us. What should we try tomorrow, Tim?"

"How about the Bronx Zoo?"

"Do you think they'll still have live animals there?"

"Very funny, Marge."

The rest of the weekend went according to script. The Bronx Zoo had a more than ample supply of live animals.

The fall foliage in Central Park was as pretty as advertised, and there were no muggers in sight. Even the New York Botanical Gardens lived up to Marge's expectations. She commented that it wasn't fair that they were expected to call it that instead of the Bronx Botanical Gardens like it used to be called. She said it was just because City Hall, and all of Manhattan for that matter, looked down on The Bronx and would have changed the name of the Bronx Zoo as well if it wasn't already so well known by that unfortunate designation.

Even Little Italy was rehabilitated, when another visitor to the Botanical Gardens, who hailed from Arthur Avenue in The Bronx's version of Little Italy, laughed at their account of Friday's restaurant misadventures. He informed them that they had totally missed the best Italian pastry in New York, which could be found right around the corner from Mulberry Street on Grand Avenue. A Sunday morning visit to Ferrarra's Bakery for cappuccino and pastries made them true believers.

The days were fine and the nights were better, but it was getting late on Sunday afternoon and it was time for Marge to go.

"I think this is my train," she said as they looked at the board next to the entrance to Track 18 at Grand Central Terminal.

"Looks like it, Marge. It's been a great weekend, but I guess it's back to reality." They kissed and she boarded the train, clutching a box of Ferrarra's cannoli under her arm.

23

TIM DECIDED THAT "DISCOVERY" was one of those legal terms used to describe a process antithetical to what it implied, like the one which says only if an order is "final" can it be appealed. As discovery progressed in the Simpson case, it seemed to him that each side asked questions or demanded documents only to prove beyond a doubt that what they already believed to be true was in fact true.

In any event, days of depositions and piles of documents shed no new light on what had happened to Rex Simpson's last Will.

Alice Tedesco's deposition produced floods of tears and repeated recesses so that she could compose herself, but nothing she said enhanced the store of shared knowledge already assembled by the warring parties. Each of the firm's partners was asked to affirm that he or she (yes, Bradford, Lord and Turner had finally removed the "glass ceiling" and now had one female partner) had not removed the Will from the office safe, or even seen the Will, for that matter.

The maid who found the late Rex in his apartment testified that the whole experience had been so horrifying that she had been suffering from nightmares ever since, that she was convinced the apartment was cursed, and that she had not returned, nor would she ever return, even if three exorcists came with her. She said the only thing she had taken after finding the body was a week-long, stay-at-home vacation to calm her shattered nerves. She suspected that Mr. Simpson had been murdered and at some point during her deposition concluded that Harold Simpson must be the murderer, that this was actually a criminal case and that Finley and his client were trying to frame her. She leaped out of the witness chair, started shrieking in a language that could not have been English, and, swinging her handbag wildly in front of her to clear the two miscreants from her path, fled the scene.

Finley, noting that this was better than the usual deposition, said "I have no further questions of this witness." Rem shrugged and said "I guess I don't either." Harold just smirked, which he had been doing a lot of.

Austin, not discouraged, predicted that Harold's deposition would be a game changer, probably even leading to withdrawal of his probate objections, since the "sniveling little worm" would have to admit that Rex wouldn't give him "cab fare to go home to Canarsie, or wherever it is he lives these days."

Rem was less sanguine about the prospects for a eureka moment. He believed Harold would concoct fantastic stories of the tragic rupture of his relationship with his brother, no doubt liberally attributing shares of the blame to parents, teachers, spouses and others who had not hesitated to destroy the sacred bond between siblings for their own misguided or selfish ends. But there would no doubt have been a miraculous turnabout, perhaps the result of a chance sidewalk encounter only a few days before Rex's untimely and totally unexpected demise. The brothers would have embraced, cried, and made their peace with one another before Rex raced joyfully back toward his apartment, vowing to make things right between them. His first act of contrition would be to tear up a "document" which he would have said he "never should have signed."

Austin looked like he'd just seen a unicorn. "He'll be under oath, Rem."

"So, who's around to contradict him? At least we can stop him from testifying at trial. With the Dead Man's Statute."

"I'm not familiar with the criminal law, Rem."

"You don't have to be. It's an evidentiary rule," Rem explained. "Harold can't testify over our objection at trial to conversations he claims to have had with his brother Rex. All I'm saying is we're not likely to get any help from him at his deposition. He's too sly for that."

"So what will we do, Rem?" asked Austin.

"I think it's time we sat down with poor Teddy Bracken again. Talk to him about whether there's any kind of a settlement he could live with."

Austin sighed in frustration, running a hand through his hair. Rem continued.

"After Harold's deposition next week, the case goes on the trial calendar, and we'll be called in for a pretrial conference. The way things are going, the court's going to push hard for a settlement. Remember, we didn't even get any help from Greg Trout's deposition, when he said the NYPD sealed the apartment after they responded to the maid's call."

He paced the room calmly, elaborating on his assessment.

"That it wasn't released until Morgan Guaranty was appointed temporary administrator of the estate. That Trout himself had personally supervised a complete search of the place before anything was removed—not even a trash basket. That there was no Will there. Not the new one, not the old one. And our friend Mickey Finn says that shows they were both destroyed—by Rex, of course. No one knows of him even having had a visitor there those last few months, other than the maid. She testified in her deposition that she never touched, much less took or discarded, any papers or other documents in the apartment."

24

"BUT IF REX DIDN'T WANT HAROLD to get anything," asked Bracken, "won't the court refuse to let us give him part of the estate?"

Tim was sitting in Rem's office with Teddy Bracken and Wolcott Denton, an attorney from another large firm who had been brought in to advise Bracken. BLT's client Morgan Guaranty was not present. Greg Trout saw no reason to be there, so long as the bank's commissions were not an issue.

"I know, Ted, maybe that's the way it should be," Rem explained. "The court may have no choice, though, if we can't prove that Rex never had the original Will. If he had it, and it's missing, and we can't prove that whatever happened to it wasn't Rex's doing, the court will have to rule that he destroyed it because he wanted to revoke it." Rem, obviously frustrated at having to deliver this message, was trying to do it as gently as possible. Turning to Denton, he said "Wally, I think we both share your client's feelings about the way the system works in these cases, but unfortunately that's what we're dealing with here."

Denton nodded, and turned to Bracken. "Ted, I can assure you that in Rem Watson you have one of the finest litigators in Manhattan handling this case. I trust his judgment implicitly. He's got to play the hand he's been dealt. And to answer your question, in my experience a court is always happy to approve a settlement agreeable to all of the parties."

Rem continued. "Ted, I can't ignore the possibility that we could lose. If that were to happen, you'd get nothing and Harold would get it all, which would be the last thing Rex would ever want. Under the circumstances, I think you should seriously consider making a generous settlement offer."

"Mr. Watson, I've never had much money anyway," said Bracken resignedly. "I don't need to be rich. I have nothing against Harold, and frankly I feel a bit sorry for him. But with all due respect to you and Mr. Denton, maybe we should just fight this all the way, win or lose. If we win, then the money will be mine, in which case I could still opt to give Harold something. This is cousin Rex's money, though, and he didn't want Harold to get any of it from him. If I agreed to go against that, I'd feel like I let Rex down. If we lose, at least we tried."

Tim was moved by Bracken's words. He thought he should be supportive. "Good for you, Mr. Bracken. Maybe things will break in our favor. You never—"

Watson cut in. "Tim, could I speak with you for a minute?" He sounded a bit annoyed. They stepped out into the corridor.

"What do you think you're doing?" he asked in a hushed tone. "This isn't a movie or a TV show. This is the real thing. And yes, it is about money. There's fifty million dollars at stake here, and right now I'm seriously worried that we might be going down on this one."

Tim thought he might faint, or perhaps go all out by having a heart attack and dying. "Oh my God, Mr. Watson. I mean, Rem. I didn't ... I thought Ted was right. He wanted to fight for something good. You know, for justice. Not that you didn't, of course. I guess I was just a little confused. I'm sorry, but—"

"We're not the rooting section at a ball game," Rem went on. "We're the lawyers, and we owe the client an honest evaluation and realistic advice. Do you think I like the idea of giving that creep Harold Simpson anything? I knew Rex Simpson, and he would have shot me if he thought I might give in to Harold. And do you think I like the idea of giving Michael Finley bragging rights about how he taught 'the Park Avenue Peacocks' a thing or two?"

"No, sir," Tim groaned.

"Tim, I like a good fight as much as the next man, but I've got to get us to the bargaining table in this case. I can't have you undermining me when I'm trying to persuade a litigant to accept what needs to be done. Maybe it would be best if you took a breather here. Why don't you work on one of your other matters while I go back in and try to bring Mr. Bracken back down to earth."

"All right, Rem. Again, I'm sorry."

"Remember, Tim, never contradict a partner in front of the client or the adversary."

Maybe this *was* the movies. Echoes of the new book *The Godfather*! Tim winced and shuffled back to his office, thinking he should probably update his resume over the weekend.

25

"WE'RE PREPARED TO MAKE a generous offer, considering the fact that our decedent made it very clear on many occasions that he wanted no part of his estate to pass to his brother," said Rem, as he and Finley sat facing Jack Zaggert in Zaggert's law department office. "None of his Wills, not one," Rem continued, "left a dime to Harold. We can prove that— we have copies of all of them. But under the circumstances, and given that his cousin Ted is not a vindictive man, and not an ungenerous man, we are willing to give Harold Simpson a million dollars, tax free, to settle his objections to the probate of the Will."

Tim sat on Rem's side of the table, having been permitted to rejoin the team after a brief exile following his faux pas during the conference with Teddy Bracken. Wally Denton was not present, but had advised Rem to call him if necessary. Tim was impressed by his boss's smooth and confident delivery of the proposal, not to mention the size of the monetary sum being discussed.

Mickey Finley obviously felt differently.

"Are you kidding me, Watson? A million? *Ten* million

would be a joke. You've got no Will. You've got no case. Copies of old Wills? You couldn't probate them even if you had the originals. They were all revoked when your guy signed the last one, and he ripped that up. My guy is his next of kin. His only heir. Blood of his blood. Flesh of—"

"Okay, okay," Zaggert interjected. "We get the picture, Mr. Finley. The court knows a lost Will is tough to probate when it was last in the possession of the decedent. From what I've heard, however, that's not necessarily a given in this case. Let's see if we can get something accomplished here today, so we don't have to put both of your clients through a trial and, who knows, maybe even an appeal. There is plenty of money here. I think we should be able to work something out."

"I don't know, your honor."

"You don't have to call me that, Mr. Finley. I'm just a member of the court's law department. Now do you have an counteroffer?"

"Let's call it a demand, Jack." Finley's transition from the formal to the familiar was swift. "We want ninety percent. That should be about forty-five million, and we'll pay our own taxes."

Tim was stunned. 45 million dollars?

This time it looked like Watson shared his opinion.

"You can't be serious, Michael" said Rem. "Where in the world did you come up with that number? Why not ask for the whole estate while you're at it?"

"Don't think I didn't consider it, but I'm trying to be reasonable here."

"Reasonable? That's outrageous. It's confiscatory."

"Confiscatory? Listen, I don't use as many fancy words as you guys, but I know what's reasonable and that's what I'm being. People who know me know Mickey Finn is a reasonable man." Finley appeared offended.

Zaggert wasn't sure he could take Finley seriously, but he figured he had better step in before this got out of hand.

"I think both of your positions are on the extreme side.

One of you wants ninety percent and the other wants ninety-eight. I guess I should be happy you're not both demanding a hundred percent and an apology of some sort, but I think we need to see some movement here. Mr. Watson, you have no Will, but Mr. Finley, you never know. That Will might just turn up one day. It's been known to happen, and I doubt you could break it if it did show up. So as things stand, you could both lose everything. Can we talk about a fifty-fifty split?"

Tim thought he saw a flicker of relief cross Rem's face, but it didn't last. Finley was on his feet.

"That won't fly. That bird won't get off the ground!" Finley bellowed, a finger in the air. "Just because I'm from the other side of the river doesn't mean I've never been in the big time. I know what my case is worth, and it's no fifty-fifty proposition."

"Mr. Finley," Zaggert tried to speak.

But Finley was just warming up. "We've got these guys by the you know what," he carried on, "and we're not letting them go until we hear them squeal. Thirty-nine million. Take it or leave it."

Apparently a counteroffer, after all.

"Thirty-nine million?" Rem furrowed his brow. "Curious number. Who gets it, you or us?"

Rem actually seemed confused, which confused Tim, who had never imagined that anything could confuse Rem Watson, but now he noticed Jack Zaggert was as confused as both of them.

"Mr. Finley, please sit down," Zaggert ordered. "Are you making a counterproposal? I assume you're not offering Mr. Watson's client thirty-nine million dollars. And by the way, Mr. Watson, I thought your client was the petitioner Morgan Guaranty. Where is Mr. Bracken's lawyer?"

"Wally Denton of the Grant Pivens firm has filed a notice of appearance on behalf of Mr. Bracken, Mr. Zaggert, but he's asked that I speak for him in these discussions. I apologize for not making that clear at the outset, but I think for now at least I can speak on Mr. Bracken's behalf in saying he's not willing to give thirty-nine million dollars to Mr. Finley's client to settle this case, assuming that's what Mr. Finley is proposing."

"Well let's assume that for the moment," Zaggert said, as he glanced at Finley who, Tim noticed, had walked over to a window and was looking out, perhaps making sure that the bird he had referred to earlier hadn't gotten off the ground. Zaggert welcomed the opportunity for a more tranquil exchange.

"I am assuming that your million dollar offer was meant only as a signal that Mr. Bracken is willing to discuss settlement. Am I correct in assuming that there is room there?"

"I think so, Mr. Zaggert, but not anything like the thirty-nine million dollars Mr. Finley indicates is his final offer."

"Mind if I smoke?" Finley was back, biting the end off his cigar.

"I'm afraid I do, Mr. Finley," responded Zaggert, somewhat icily. "And city ordinances forbid it in any event. I assume they extend to Kings County as well?"

"There you go. Acting like Brooklyn isn't part of the civilized world, like there's no intelligent life on the other side of the Brooklyn Bridge. Well, listen. I've won a few cases in my lifetime, and I think I'm going to win this one. If you guys aren't ready to talk turkey, I might as well head back to the jungle with my client."

Zaggert's face flushed.

"Please sit down, Mr. Finley." His voice cracked a bit. "I meant no offense. Perhaps I'm a little tired. I apologize, but let's see if we can get these discussions back on track."

Finley looked at him.

"Why don't we take a short break," Zaggert said, "while the two of you speak to your clients? Mr. Watson, you may want to give Mr. Denton a call as well. Then come back in, let's say in half an hour, and we'll see if we're any closer. And Mr. Watson, I'd like to hear a better number from your man when we resume."

"A number like thirty-nine million," said Finley, waving his unlit cigar in the air as he exited the room.

26

"HE WOULDN'T COME DOWN more than that? Are you sure?" asked Chamberlain. Watson, Trout, Bracken, Denton and Tim also sat at the table in one of the conference rooms at BLT. A generous offering of pastries, juices, coffee and ice water was laid out on a credenza along the wall, but from the undisturbed look of it, no one had much of an appetite that morning. Tim still felt as if he were on supervised probation with at best a tenuous hold on his job. Mostly, though, he felt sorry for poor Teddy Bracken, who looked miserable and totally out of place.

"Rem, you say he started at forty-five million and has come down four times since," said Austin. "First to thirty-nine million, then to thirty-six million, then to thirty-three million, and now to thirty million. Where did those numbers come from?"

Even Tim knew the answer to that one, but he kept his mouth shut.

"Who knows how Finley thinks," replied Watson, "but it's pretty clear he's not coming down any further."

"How high have we gone?" Trout asked, glancing at Teddy, who looked away.

"We finally agreed to the law assistant's proposal of a fifty-fifty split, so twenty-five million," Rem replied. "Wally feels that Ted is inclined to go to thirty and be done with it. After taxes, fees and commissions, that would leave about ten million for him. Am I right on that, Wally?"

Denton looked at Bracken, who nodded glumly.

"That's correct, Rem, but he and I will be going over the details once more before the next court appearance. He's feeling a little badly about the whole thing right now and I think he could use a few days to let it settle in."

Tim wondered if he would ever be in a position where he could be glum about receiving 10 million dollars.

Denton excused himself to attend another meeting. Bracken followed him out. When both were gone, Austin vented his frustration.

"Ten million, when Rex wanted him to have it all. What a disgrace," said Austin. "And I suppose poor Harold would walk away with fifteen?"

"I think ten," ventured Tim, without thinking. He immediately wondered whether he had once again, and probably for the last time, violated the prohibition against contradicting a BLT partner in front of a client.

But Austin was apparently not protected by the rule, since Rem actually seemed slightly amused by Tim's comment, and asked him to elaborate.

"Well Austin, I may be wrong, but I think Mickey Finley most likely took this case on a contingency. Probably one-third. So I'd guess he'd get ten of the thirty, leaving Harold with twenty, or ten after taxes. I think that's why all of his offers were divisible by three."

"Why, that ambulance chasing con artist," Austin nearly squealed. "Rem, I meant what I said. We really should file a grievance. This kind of person leaves a stain on the profession."

"Actually, there's no ethical issue involved in that type of fee arrangement, Austin," Rem corrected him. "Mickey Finn might be a little short on subtlety, but he's good at arithmetic. I think we can all safely assume that the fee arrangement has been the driving force behind the numbers he's been putting on the table. Not everyone can pay our hourly rates, you know. The man in the street might find $250 per hour for your time and $350 for mine to be a little too steep for his budget. Access to justice could be denied for many if it were not for contingent fees, which only have to be reasonable under the circumstances. I think Tim's theory is spot on."

Tim was ecstatic, but wondered if Austin would consider his familiarity with this type of fee arrangement to be a dangerous sign of a socialist streak in his character. His reverie was quickly broken by Trout.

"What about our commissions, Rem?" asked Trout. "My shop has accrued a million dollars as our anticipated executor's commission here. It's actually going to be a few thousand more than that under the new statute, but we rounded it down so as not to look silly when the auditors come around."

Tim was starting to feel out of his league again.

"That's covered, Greg. Finley would agree to Morgan Guaranty serving as administrator by designation. I don't think he trusts his client any more than we would when it comes to handling money. After all, as Tim points out, Finley has a significant financial stake in this himself."

Tim's spirits rose again, pride swelling in his chest. He was starting to like this.

"So if you're all on board," Rem continued, "I think we should take the deal. None of us likes what happened here, but I think we have to stomach it. As Wally mentioned before he left, Teddy will take a few days to sort things out in his own mind and then speak privately with Wally before we finalize things. They have an appointment on Monday. Then we're due back in court next Thursday, where we'll put the settlement on the record if we're all in accord."

Reassured about his employer's compensation, Trout

believed compliments were in order. "Well, good job then, Rem. You've represented us well under what I'm sure have been very trying circumstances. And Wolcott Denton? He's first class. We have excellent relationships with several of his firm's clients. I'm sure he'll serve Mr. Bracken well."

Or serve Trout's bank well, Tim thought to himself. Bracken's desire to fight for his cousin Rex' wishes was one thing, but a settlement that assured Morgan Guaranty a million-dollar commission—or a million plus a few thousand, to be precise—was not to be taken lightly.

27

"I CAN'T BELIEVE HOW SMUG Harold Simpson acted in court,"
Tim recounted, sipping a beer at their regular table in
Smokey's. Marge listened with her usual intensity. "He even
gets a break on the estate taxes. They'd be seventy-seven percent on most of the estate, and that's just federal, but a lot of
the money was in family trusts, and that part goes tax free."

"Who gets the trusts?"

"Well, Rex had the right to name the beneficiary in his
Will, so he named Ted Bracken. If the Will goes down, they
stay in the family. In other words, they'd go to Harold. He's
the closest relative."

"Tax free?"

"Tax free. Anyway, Harold was so cocky, couldn't stop
smirking. Not that he tried very hard. You'd think he'd be
at least a little nervous. He's so close to becoming filthy rich
when he could be living in flop houses and standing on bread
lines. I mean, what if the Will shows up at the eleventh hour?
Found under the refrigerator or something?"

"It's not going to show up, Tim. I told you, somebody
stole it."

"How can you know that Marge? Why would anyone do such a thing, even if they did have access to the office safe? The partners certainly wouldn't do it. It's already an embarrassment to the firm and it's going to get worse once word of this settlement gets out."

"You mean there's no confidentiality agreement?"

"No. Rem tried, but Finley wouldn't go for it. He said he knew 'a thing or two about the Constitution,' and that 'the public has an absolute right to know what goes on in our courts.' He also prattled on about freedom of speech and a few other things his new intern must have looked up for him. Anyway, Jack Zaggert put the nail in the coffin by saying there would be no confidentiality agreement even with the parties' consent, since the surrogate didn't like to seal litigation files, so we should all move on. It was pretty obvious that Mickey Finley plans to issue a press release when the case is over, so he was delighted. I think his intern might be in for a raise."

"I thought his intern was working for nothing? Isn't that what Finley told you when you turned down the paying job?"

"Right. Well maybe a desk or a chair then."

"Tim, how much time do we have to find the Will?"

"Are you kidding? Today's Friday. I want to see my father this weekend and to spend some time with you, as we planned. The case is on next Thursday to pick a trial date, absent a settlement. And I have no idea whether the Will still exists, much less where it might be if it does."

"I'm an investigator, Tim. I know that Will was stolen. Austin Chamberlain may be something of a buffoon, but this is his area, tax and estate planning, and even you say he's good at it and respected in the field. He knows how important it is to safeguard his clients' original Wills, especially clients as wealthy and well known as Rex Simpson."

A roar erupted from the bar area. The usual revelers and Toots were there, obviously enjoying some entertaining subject much lighter than the impossible-to-answer questions surrounding Rex Simpson's Will. Tim glanced at the group, then turned back to Marge.

"Here we are," he said to her. "Same place, different time, still trying to solve the same mystery. You said it was up to me to figure it out, but I haven't. So tell me, what happened?"

"He would never have put the old Will back in the safe instead of the new one." Marge leaned in as she spoke. "But he could very well have scribbled his name in the 'Returned' column next to the entry for the old Will by mistake. Some of the most brilliant people are like absentminded professors when it comes to day-to-day drudgery, plus Austin is only book smart, not brilliant. And if it really was the old Will and not the new one that went back in, where did the old one go? Neither Will was in the safe when Alice Tedesco went looking for them. No, Chamberlain retrieved the new Will by mistake, returned it when he realized what had happened, and then removed the old one so Rem Watson could send that one back to the client. He marked the old one down as the one he had returned, and everyone's been going crazy ever since."

"So, where's the new one?"

"I told you, someone stole it."

Tim was getting tired of this.

"Fine. Suppose you're right. The new Will went back to the safe, at least for a while, and then someone took it. Who? Alice Tedesco? I think she'd swallow a cyanide capsule before anyone compromised the sanctity of that safe."

"I agree. Alice didn't do it. Not from what you've told me about her."

"Then who did?"

"Let's run down our list of suspects. Assume Austin Chamberlain put the Will back in the safe, or that he had Alice Tedesco do it. By the way, do the partners actually do this themselves? Or do they ask her to do it?"

"I think they ask her. They probably call her, rather than making the trip down to the file room themselves. Most of them probably don't even know the combination to the safe, and frankly, most of them don't do much estate work."

"How are these sign in, sign out rules enforced?"

"If the partner doesn't personally take a Will out of the safe, the partner is still required to sign for it when Alice delivers it to the partner's office. She brings the log book for signature when she delivers the Will."

"And when it's returned?"

"Same thing. The partner either brings it back to her and signs the book there—that's what Austin did—or asks her to come get the Will and then signs the book when she picks it up."

"And that's it? No one else has access to the safe?"

"No. Except Tom Quinn, of course. He even knows the combination, so he can cover for Alice when she's on vacation or out sick."

"Did Quinn sign one of those affidavits Finley asked for?"

"Not that I know of."

"Why not?"

"I don't know. I guess he's sort of inconspicuous. Everyone takes him for granted. It's a shame, actually. He's a nice man and really knows what he's doing. They'll probably miss him a lot when he retires."

"He's planning on retiring?

"Last week I heard someone say that he was leaving at the end of the year."

Marge stared at Tim.

28

"HE DIED? WHEN?" Tim felt a cold tingling sensation spreading through his chest and shoulders as he asked Mike Green the question. They were in Tim's office, where Mike had just stopped by to share the news.

"Yesterday, apparently. One of the associates was in doing some prep work for a deposition that's scheduled for today. He saw Tom at his desk at around 5:30. I guess he's the last person to have seen him alive. The messengers on the early shift found him slumped over his desk when they showed up for work this morning at seven. They tried calling that new 911 number, but it didn't work, so they called the police. When the ambulance came, he was already gone."

Mike seemed more excited than upset. Tim supposed things like this didn't happen very often in these sedate quarters. And, as Mike said, "Tom was pretty old, probably over sixty. They say it was a heart attack. He'd been having some health problems lately, and that was one of the reasons he was planning to retire."

"Do they know what he was doing here on a Sunday?"

"No. I only heard about it a few minutes ago, but no

one's sure what brought him in here. They did say there were a lot of papers on his desk that he might have been going over, but nothing that seemed pressing. I mean, none of that estate stuff is ever pressing, right?"

Tim wasn't so sure about that, his main exposure to "estate stuff" having been the Simpson Estate, but he didn't see any point in questioning Mike's opinion.

"They removed the body right away, so I didn't get to see it, but it must have been quite a sight. Can you imagine if someone got a quick shot off with his Polaroid and gave it to the Daily News? 'Lawyer dies at his desk! Gives his last full measure of strength to the firm he served for forty years! Dies with his boots on! AFL/CIO calls for unionization of overworked associates at big Wall Street firms!' It wouldn't be as good as if it were some twenty-six-year-old associate croaking after another hundred hour work week, but still."

Mike was warming to his subject, but Tim was having a hard time focusing.

"Did any of those papers have anything to do with the Simpson Estate?"

"What papers?"

"The ones you said were on Tom's desk when they found him."

"I don't know. Why?"

"Well, I'm working on that case, and I just thought—"

"You'll have to ask the secretary they sent in to organize everything. She's working with Chamberlain, since I guess he'll have to figure out who should pick up from Quinn on his matters. Anyway, I'd better get going. Gotta take care of the living, after all. They're the ones who pay my salary."

"Okay, Mike. Thanks for letting me know. I think it's very sad."

"Right. See ya."

Tim dialed Marge's number.

"Conley Investigations. Marge here."

"Marge, it's Tim."

"What's up, Tim?"

"Tom Quinn is dead."

"What?" She paused. "When? How?"

"He died at his desk over the weekend. Apparent heart attack. No one seems to know what he was doing in the office."

"So you won't be talking to him."

"Obviously not. And now I don't know what to do."

"The Simpson case is still on for Thursday?"

"I assume so. Tom was a law school classmate of Rex Simpson, but he wasn't working on the estate."

"Oh boy! Let me think about this. We'll have to come up with a plan B. I'll call you back later."

Marge hung up just as an interoffice memo was dropped on Tim's desk by one of the messengers:

"It is with great sadness that I report to you this morning the sudden and tragic death of our beloved friend and associate, Tom Quinn. Tom has been a stalwart figure here at Bradford, Lord and Turner for over forty years, and was a source of inspiration and support to every one of us who has had the pleasure and honor to work with him during his tenure at the firm. I, for one, am deeply grateful for having had that opportunity. He was a fine professional, in the best sense of the word.

"Tom's family has informed us that there will be a wake at the McCulloch Funeral Home in Bay Ridge tomorrow and Wednesday. Viewing hours will be from 2PM to 5PM and from 7PM to 9PM both days. A funeral Mass will be celebrated at St. Patrick's Church on Fourth Avenue in Bay Ridge on Thursday at 10 AM. All of you are invited to pay your respects. In lieu of flowers, contributions to the Legal Aid Society are suggested.

Rem Watson"

The phone rang and Tim picked it up.

"Marge?"

"Tim?" It was Rem.

"Yes, this is Tim."

"It's Rem. Terrible tragedy, Tim. I just wanted to tell you that Thursday's off in the Simpson case. It's been rescheduled for next week—Thursday the thirteenth. Zaggert is tied up until then, but he was very accommodating. He knew Tom for years—said he was one of the finest gentlemen he's ever had dealings with over at the court. He not only understood our wish to attend Tom's funeral, but plans to attend himself. He said Mickey Finley will just have to wait a bit longer to start his victory celebration."

Grateful for the reprieve, Tim thanked Rem. He was about to get off the phone when he had another thought.

"Rem?"

"Yes?"

"Mike Green told me about Tom Quinn this morning. He said Tom was working on a stack of papers when it happened. What could have been so important that he had to come in on a Sunday?"

"We're all wondering about that, actually. No one is aware of any looming deadlines that Tom had to meet, and the strangest thing is that some of the notes on his desk related to the Simpson Estate, and he wasn't even working on that, as you know. I'll have someone bring them down to you, so you can put them in the file. I'd better run. I'll talk to you about Simpson next week."

A few minutes later, a messenger walked into Tim's office and handed him a thin folder with the word "Simpson" written across the top edge.

"Mr. Watson's secretary said to give this to you."

"Thanks," said Tim. The young man started to leave.

"By the way," Tim called out.

The messenger turned around.

"I'm Tim O'Leary. It's nice to meet you." He offered a handshake.

"Stan Kowalczyk," said the messenger, a bit startled. He shook Tim's hand.

"Well, thanks for bringing the folder," said Tim.

"Um, sure. Anytime."

As the young man departed, Tim made a mental note to learn the names of all of these anonymous staff members who were generally ignored around the office. He wondered whether Tom Quinn had felt the sting of being taken for granted. He suspected that he had.

The folder contained only a few pages. There was a copy of a statute, a check number, and a handwritten note reading, "$3 to Clerk, Surrogate's Court." Quinn had also written a date of a "receipt" of some sort, and the address of Simpson's Manhattan apartment, followed by a question mark. Then there was what looked like a telephone number that Tim didn't remember having seen in the estate file. He picked up the phone and called Marge, who answered on the first ring.

"The case has been put over for one week so everyone can go to the funeral," he told her.

"That's a break, but I haven't come up with any ideas yet. You?"

"Well, it's sort of strange. They found a folder on Tom Quinn's desk that was marked 'Simpson.'"

"You just told me he wasn't working on that."

"He wasn't. And nothing in the folder seems to have anything to do with the probate proceeding." Tim described the contents to her.

"What's the statute about?" she asked.

"It has to do with the safekeeping of Wills in court."

"Could the check number actually be a court file number?"

"No. It's different."

"So how do you know it's a check number?"

"Because it says 'check number.'"

"How about the other number, could that be a file number?"

Tim looked at the page again. "No, it doesn't say 'file number.'"

"That doesn't prove anything."

This was starting to get annoying.

"I know it doesn't, Marge, but it's not one of our office's file numbers—the format is different—and it's not the file number assigned to the Simpson Estate by the Surrogate's Court when we filed the probate petition. Actually, it looks more like a phone number. It even starts with an area code—212—but then the rest of the number can't be a phone number because it starts with a 'one.'"

"Are you sure it's a one, and not a seven?"

"Listen, Marge, I don't know what any of this means. I just know that I can't talk to Quinn anymore, not that I was sure I would have had the nerve to do it in the first place, and I wouldn't dare talk to Rem about your theory. Not after the last time I put my foot in my mouth with him."

"Are you going to Quinn's wake?"

"Yes. I can't go tomorrow, but I'm going to try to get there on Wednesday night. Then I'd like to go to the funeral on Thursday."

"Could I meet you there?"

"You want to go to the funeral?"

"Yes. And then maybe we can do a little detective work."

— 29 —

BAY RIDGE WAS IN THE "IT'S STILL OKAY" category in the lexicon of native New Yorkers who had grown up in the outer boroughs. They generally rated sections of the city by how similar a neighborhood was to what it had been like when they were children. If the person was Irish and Catholic, and came from a neighborhood populated by other "Hibernian mackerel snappers," then it was "still okay" if it was still full of similar folk. Modest exceptions were made for certain nationalities and ethnic groups, so long as they were of the same color or didn't flaunt their differences, such as by wearing turbans or burkas or by flashing peace signs at strangers. As World War II veterans moved out to the suburbs with their families and that type of thing occurred, the neighborhood was said to have "gone downhill." This was apparently the case even if the streets were clean, the apartments and houses were well maintained, and the places of worship were still in full operation, albeit utilizing different rites and symbols to worship the same deity.

Tim had lived, worked, and studied in Manhattan, which was after all a borough, although not thought of as one by those who lived and worked there. They referred to it simply as "the city," and many entered the other boroughs only when passing through them by train or car. Beyond sleeping at his uncle's apartment in Queens, Tim had little if any notion of what these "boroughs" were all about as his subway rumbled along toward Brooklyn. He was on the "N" train, which he had been told to leave for the "R" train at 59th Street, even though he had gotten on the "N" train at 59th Street in the first place when he began his trip. That was because there were two 59th Streets, one in Manhattan and one in Brooklyn. The latter had presumably insisted on retaining its right to name its own streets when it became part of New York City in 1898, after which its citizens had chronic second thoughts and regularly threatened to secede from this union. Many Brooklynites asserted that the merger had resulted in their being treated as a second-class borough—or so said Ken Clark. He lived in upscale Brooklyn Heights, which was close enough to Manhattan geographically and culturally to be deemed an acceptable habitat. Not realizing that there was a significant distinction to be drawn between Brooklyn Heights in particular and Brooklyn in general, Tim had approached Clark for directions to Bay Ridge. In the process of responding, Ken provided Tim with this historical background. He also extended an invitation to see a "delightful string quartet" performing selections from Mendelssohn's String Concerto in E Minor. The recital would take place on Friday evening at historic Trinity Church in lower Manhattan. Tim was able to decline with secret relief, given Marge's upcoming visit to attend the funeral, and then maybe to stay on for the weekend.

Tim found himself pleasantly surprised as the train unexpectedly emerged from the darkness of the tunnel, climbed up to a bridge and crossed what he assumed was the East River, which separated Manhattan from Brooklyn. The view of the Manhattan skyline behind him, the Brooklyn Bridge to his right and downtown Brooklyn ahead was stunning, but his fellow passengers seemed not to notice. They were absorbed in their copies of the New York Post or the Daily News, or just dozing as the train rolled across the bridge and plunged back into a tunnel on the other side of the river.

The other riders remained transfixed by their personal distractions, notwithstanding the opening of the door at one end of the subway car, and the appearance of a rumpled, grizzled man entering from the next car. He wore sunglasses and tapped a white cane ahead of him as he shuffled down the aisle, holding a cup and wearing a sign suspended from his neck that proclaimed "Blind, Hungry and Homeless." Tim marveled at how the poor soul was able to maintain his balance as the train lurched and swayed. His fellow travelers, however, looked either indifferent or annoyed as they pulled in their feet so the blind fellow could pass. Reaching into his pocket, Tim found a few coins and dropped them into the beggar's cup, wondering how New Yorkers could be so callous. Hearing the clink of the coins, the blind man turned toward Tim. "Bless you, young man," he murmured, and continued on down the aisle. Someone standing near Tim chuckled, "How do you suppose he knew you were a man?" The other zombies looked up, laughed, and lapsed back into their catatonic states.

The subway hurtled on until it reached Brooklyn's version of 59th Street. More than half of the passengers awoke from their reveries and bolted for the doors. Tim, caught up in the migration, moved with the crowd to the platform just as another train with a large "R" rolled down the track on the opposite side. When the "R" train stopped and opened its doors, the crowd surged forward, carrying Tim with them into the car. Once inside, they immediately returned to their previous diversions.

By the time the train reached the 95th Street station, Tim was practically alone, it being the end of the line. He stepped out onto a platform that was nearly deserted, and very unlike anything he had experienced in the jammed Manhattan stations where all of the passengers usually seemed to be late for wherever they were going.

When he reached the top of the stairs and stepped onto the sidewalk, it was still light and he was struck by the calmness of his surroundings. There were buses and cars and people, just like in Manhattan, but so many fewer than there, and it was so much quieter here. He actually noticed the sky and the light, and even though it was fairly breezy, there wasn't the bone chilling wind-tunnel effect of the corridors between the Manhattan skyscrapers. Here the breeze was just that. It didn't make him want to get indoors as quickly as his feet would take him. This was nice.

Tim walked down Fourth Avenue, wondering if the neighborhood would be so peaceful when they completed the construction of the Verrazano Bridge. He hoped so.

Arriving at the McCulloch Funeral Home, Tim went inside. A sign in the lobby directed him to "Parlor B" for the Thomas Quinn wake. When he entered the room, he found only a few people there. Quinn was lying in an open casket at the front of the room. The handful of visitors were standing about talking with one another and, as seemed to be the case at most of these events, ignoring the guest of honor.

Tim approached the casket and knelt before it. Tom appeared somewhat different from the living version, but not appreciably so. His face was peaceful, and he wore a charcoal-grey suit and blue tie which Tim had seen him in a number of times at the office. Tim prayed briefly for Quinn's soul, and then for his help—in case by chance Quinn was listening—in finding the last Will of Rex Simpson. Then he rose and turned to see an older woman looking at him.

"Hello, young man." This time coming from someone not purporting to be sightless. "I am Catherine Quinn, Tom's wife. Are you from the office?"

"Yes, Mrs. Quinn. I am. My name is Tim O'Leary. I'm very sorry for your loss."

"Oh, you're the young man Tom spoke about. He said

you reminded him very much of himself when he started out. He said he hoped the firm had come along far enough to give you more of a chance than he ever had. He was never one of them."

"One of them?"

"Tom felt that he was passed over because his ordinary Irish-American heritage wouldn't appeal to the wealthy old-line families that gravitated toward the firm for their estate planning needs. Bradford was much more likely to select their estates partners from the ranks of socially-connected lawyers like Austin Chamberlain and Kensington Clark. I tried to remind Tom that he shouldn't let himself become bitter, but I'm not sure that I always succeeded."

"I'm sorry, Mrs. Quinn. I really don't know how those things work, but I'm not even from an Ivy League law school, like your husband was. And they hired me."

"There have been changes over the years, Tim. But by the time they took hold, it was really too late for my Tom to be made partner, even though we both hoped he would."

She looked away for a moment, then set her jaw and continued.

"It really wasn't right, you know. Tom gave that office his whole life. What did he have to show for it in the end? A little life insurance policy and a tiny pension for when he planned to retire later this year? I kept asking him what we were going to live on. And what with our son dying in Egypt during that Suez Crisis in '57 and leaving his two children behind! Who was going to send them to college? Their mother has nothing." She paused for a breath, but seemed nowhere near finishing her indictment of the tight-fisted firm of Bradford, Lord and Turner.

Tim was starting to feel warm, and sweat began to trickle down his back as he glanced around the room for any familiar face who might give him an excuse to break free. Mrs. Quinn had obviously not been the person best equipped to keep her late spouse from journeying down the road to bitterness.

"I told him he was too easygoing, that plenty of other firms would jump at the chance to get him if he'd only reach out to them. That would have put the fear of God into the exalted powers-that-be at Bradford, Lord and T!"

Tim suspected that he was not the first to hear this bit of poetry. He glanced over to the casket's occupant who, he thought, might have nodded in agreement had he still possessed the ability.

"But no, not Tom. He never would. And lately there was this new thing—he was going to retire, and everything was going to be all right. We'd be fine and the grandkids could go to college. We'd celebrate with a vacation in Myrtle Beach. Maybe even get a place in Florida after that. Really, I thought he was losing his mind. And now this."

Her voice finally broke, and she started to sob. Heads turned and sympathetic looks flowed in her direction. The now slowly-growing crowd of mourners assumed that the widow Quinn was overcome by grief at the sudden loss of her soul mate. Several moved to comfort her, and Tim, gratefully, made his escape.

He noticed Ken Clark enter the room, and went over to say hello.

"Oh. Hi, Tim. How were the directions?" Clark seemed pleased to see him.

"Perfect. No problem at all. And I enjoyed the walk from the station. It's so quiet and low key here compared to Manhattan. This is my first visit to this part of Brooklyn."

"Well, this neighborhood is better than Bed Stuy and East New York, I suppose. But the Heights is about as far into the borough as I like to venture," said Clark drily. He was obviously of the opinion that the mere absence of gunshots did not qualify a neighborhood as a desirable environment for the more civilized of New Yorkers. "I'll be heading back there as soon as I pay my respects. How is poor Mrs. Quinn faring?"

"She's doing fairly well, I think," said Tim, hoping he

sounded convincing. "Maybe just a little dazed by the suddenness of it."

"Actually, Tim, this is not for publication, but I heard she gave some of the partners a bit of a hard time on the phone yesterday. Apparently she was under the impression that her husband had a lot bigger balance in his retirement account than she was told when she called. She insisted that he was supposed to be getting a sizable chunk of money as part of his retirement. She even threatened to hire a lawyer if they persisted in—her word—'lying' about her entitlement." Ken looked across the room. "Well, I guess I'd better suck it up and go speak to her."

Clark started to move away, but Tim held him back for a moment.

"Ken, I think you know I'm working on the Simpson Estate litigation. You do some estates work as well as corporate, so you might be able to explain something to me. Tom had a file folder marked 'Simpson' on his desk, and I'm trying to figure out why a copy of a statute was in it."

"What statute?" Clark turned back, looking relieved at this brief reprieve from his condolence call on Mrs. Quinn.

"It was section 2507 of the SCPA. Titled 'Reception of wills for safekeeping.'"

"Oh, that's the 'Poor Man's Will Safe.' It lets people deposit original Wills in the Surrogate's Court for safekeeping, but nobody ever does, at least nobody I know."

"So if someone does do it, what happens to the Will when the person who signed it dies?" asked Tim.

"Well, that's the problem. If the person's attorney is the one who put it there, he tells the family. Tries to get them to hire him so he can start a probate proceeding. That is, if the attorney is still around. Most lawyers hold onto the Will themselves, or give the document to the client when he signs it.

"The few who put their clients' Wills in the court usually do it years after the signing ceremony, because they're retiring. They don't want to go to the trouble of trying to contact the clients, especially since a lot of clients move after signing their Wills and never bother to tell the lawyer. If they know where the clients are, of course, they'd never put the Wills in court, because there are filing fees involved. They just tell the clients to come and get their Wills or else."

"Or else what?"

"Or else they'll be discarded, I guess. I don't know. As I said, we don't do that."

"So what happens when a client whose Will was filed in the court dies, and the family finds this attorney's name in the client's papers? I assume that they try to contact him about the Will, but what if they find out the attorney has died?"

"They're screwed."

"That's it?"

"Well, if they're lucky and someone guesses what might have happened, they go check the Surrogate's Court in the county where the relative lived. At least where he lived before moving in with his daughter, or into the nursing home. In other words, where he lived when he might have signed a Will with that lawyer. They ask the clerk whether there's a Will on file."

"And if they don't think to do that?"

"Then some archeologist will be very excited a few thousand years from now, when digging down and stumbling upon the vault of the Surrogate's Court, and finding the Will. He'll write a doctoral thesis on why lawyers used to say 'I, Sally Smith, being of sound and disposing mind and memory, now domiciled in the City, County and State of New York, and aware of the uncertainty of this life, and not being under any restraint, do hereby make, publish and declare this to be my Last Will and Testament, hereby revoking all Wills and Codicils heretofore made by me,' instead of just saying 'I am Sally Smith, and this is my Will.' Proving the theory, of course, that lawyers in the twentieth century were the primary cause of the deforestation of the planet, through their use of ridiculously excessive verbiage that required tons of paper from billions of trees that could just as easily have been left standing in the forest."

"I still don't get it, though. What does section 2507 have to do with the Simpson Estate?"

"I haven't the slightest idea. You'd have to ask Tom," chuckled Clark, as he moved off to "pay his respects" to Tom Quinn's widow.

30

THURSDAY MORNING WAS A PERFECT DAY for a funeral—grey, cold and rainy. Tim closed his umbrella as he walked up the front steps of St. Patrick's Church. He looked at his watch. It was about 9:45 so he was early, but Marge, whom he was supposed to meet in front of the church, was nowhere in sight. He went inside to get out of the rain, imagining Marge would do the same when she arrived. Remembering something his mother had told him many years before, Tim slipped into one of the pews in the back of the church. He knelt down, closed his eyes, and silently made three wishes. He had hardly finished articulating the third when he felt someone kneel down beside him.

"What are you doing back here, Tim?" whispered Marge. "Don't they hold funerals in the front of the church?"

"I was making three wishes."

"You were doing what?"

"My mother always told my sisters and me that you got three free wishes every time you went into a church you had never visited before."

"You believe that?"

"I'm not sure. But why squander the chance if it might be true?"

"Let me know if it works. What did you wish for?"

"I can't tell you. If I do, they won't come true."

"This is a side of you I didn't know about, Tim. Do you still believe in Santa Claus?"

"Maybe we should change the subject, Marge." Tim blushed, hoping the light in the back of the church was too dim for her to notice.

"Good idea. And while we're at it, let's move up closer to the front. There aren't that many people up there. I don't think it's going to be a sellout." It looked like Marge was in her wise guy private detective mode today.

Tim and Marge walked up toward the altar and sat down in a pew several rows from the front. A few dozen people were already seated, and more came up the aisle as the minutes passed. Tim recognized some attorneys and staff from the office, and saw Jack Zaggert arriving. He sat down a few rows away, and Tim discreetly pointed him out to Marge, mentioning his involvement in the Simpson case. He also identified others he had told her about, but she acknowledged their presence dismissively.

"The only one I'd like to meet isn't here yet," whispered Marge.

"Who would that be?"

"Mrs. Quinn, of course."

Just then, the organist, who had taken his place in the balcony, struck up a somber dirge. A casket surrounded by six pallbearers began moving up the aisle. Mrs. Quinn followed, holding hands with an attractive pair of teenagers who, Tim assumed, were the grandchildren she had told him about at the wake. The procession moved slowly to the front of the church, where the family members were met by a priest who sprinkled the casket with holy water as the service began.

"I'm not sure if she's sad or angry," whispered Marge.

"Could be a little of both. You do have to feel sorry for her."

"I guess you're right. Maybe I'm being a little mean today. I probably put my game face on too early. Sorry."

"It's okay, Marge. I think we're both getting weirded out by this thing."

"I know. It's creepy. And, Tim, I hope your three wishes come true."

31

OUTSIDE THE CHURCH, Mrs. Quinn entered a limousine with her two grandchildren, along with a woman around 40 years old whom Tim assumed was their mother. The funeral director closed the car doors for them, and turned to the mourners who milled around at the bottom of the church steps. There would be no trip to the cemetery that morning, as the family was to have a private graveside service later. The rain had stopped, but the sky was still grey and the air still chilly.

The funeral director was clearly a man accustomed to these situations. He addressed them formally but pleasantly.

"The family appreciates your coming today, and invites you to join them for lunch at Chadwick's Restaurant. It's just a few blocks from here on Third Avenue. I have directions for anyone who needs them." He started to pass out small sheets of paper. Tim and Marge took one, glanced at it, and decided it was close enough to walk, even if the rain did start up again. 10 minutes later they arrived at the restaurant, a traditional American, Sunday-dinner style establishment, and went in. A woman greeted them as they entered and asked if they were with the Quinn party. After confirming that to be the case, she led them to a private room nearby, wished them an enjoyable lunch and returned to her post by the door. Catherine Quinn was already in the room as they entered. She was chatting with several of her contemporaries. Marge walked straight toward her, and Tim hurried to catch up.

"Good morning, Mrs. Quinn," said Tim, a bit flustered as he stepped in front of Marge. "I don't know if you remember me from yesterday evening. I'm Tim O'Leary, from your husband's office. This is my friend Marge Conley."

"Of course, I remember you, Mr. O'Leary," said Mrs. Quinn, much calmer than she had been the night before. Tim hoped it would last. "And it's a pleasure to meet you, Miss Conley. I assume it's 'Miss.' Am I right? Oh, I'm so old-fashioned. It's probably 'Ms.' Isn't that what you young women are starting to call yourselves?"

"Either way, Mrs. Quinn, but I wish you'd call me Marge. And I'm very sorry for your loss. Tim spoke very highly of Mr. Quinn. His passing must have been quite a shock."

"Oh, it was. It was. And at such a terrible time. I don't know if your Timothy told you, but Mr. Quinn and I were planning on his retiring soon. He was going to receive a handsome severance from the firm so we could live comfortably afterwards, but now they're reneging and ..." Mrs. Quinn choked up just as she was starting to build up a head of steam again.

Tim tugged Marge's sleeve, looking for escape routes. Marge ignored him.

"That's terrible, Mrs. Quinn. May I call you Catherine?"

"My friends call me 'Kitty.'"

"Then Kitty it is. But 'severance'? Isn't that when someone is let go?"

"Oh, I don't know, dear. Maybe that's the wrong word for it. I really don't understand these things." Tim was struck by how quickly she had calmed down again. Marge's characterization of the firm's duplicity as "terrible" must have done the trick. He decided he had better stick around and see where this was going.

Marge went on in her soothing manner. "What did Mr. Quinn call it, do you remember?"

"Oh, he didn't give it a name, actually. He just said there would be a lot of money—more than a few hundred thousand dollars—coming in soon."

"Did he say from where?"

"He didn't really say, so I asked him if it was coming from the firm. They certainly owed him."

"And what did he tell you?"

"He just said 'You might say that,' and then sort of laughed."

"Are you sure you didn't misunderstand him?"

"Absolutely not," Kitty bristled. "I was so surprised that they were finally going to do the right thing by us that I asked him again, several times. After awhile he'd become annoyed, and he finally started making a joke out of it, I think to shut me up. But I could see he was tense. He was probably worried that they wouldn't keep their promise. Oh, how right he was. When he died and I called them to ask about the payment, they said they had no idea what I was talking about. They acted like I was crazy." She began to weep.

Marge put her arm around the sobbing woman's shoulders and led her over to one of the chairs that were positioned near the wall. Others looked on sympathetically, but held back. After all, why intrude on a situation that seemed under control? Tim felt pretty much the same way, but didn't think Marge would appreciate him abandoning her at this point, so he followed along. She had helped Mrs. Quinn into the chair and was kneeling before her, speaking soothingly and offering her a tissue which she had magically obtained somewhere along the way.

"Now, now Kitty. Be brave," Marge was saying as Tim came closer. "If they promised your Tom something like that, they will have to pay it. Maybe you should get a lawyer."

Tim almost collapsed. Was she trying to get him fired?

"Marge?" he uttered quietly.

"Well I have heard that they're scared to death of this one they call Mickey Finn," said Kitty, not crying anymore. "Maybe you're right. I should give him a call."

Tim slumped into a nearby chair, doomed. Marge forged on.

"There, Kitty. See what I mean? Things aren't always as bad as they appear. There's always hope. By the way, one thing you said before made me wonder. You said Mr. Quinn started making a joke out of it. What did you mean by that?"

"It wasn't funny to me, but he kept it up. First he started saying things like the countdown to 'payday' would start soon. Then one day he actually started what he called 'the official countdown.' I told him he was upsetting me, but he wouldn't stop."

"The payday. Did it arrive yet?" asked Marge.

Kitty turned a bit pale. "Now that you mention it, it would have been today. Today of all days. What a cruel joke." She dropped her head and her shoulders heaved. Marge proffered another tissue and stood up, as one of the other guests finally came to help. Marge and Tim both patted Mrs. Quinn's shoulders, and moved away.

Tim wondered whether he should approach Jack Zaggert to see if there were any job openings at the Surrogate's Court. He looked around the room hoping Zaggert had accepted the invitation to lunch.

"Now we're getting somewhere!" Marge was standing in front of him, unaccountably ebullient. "Did you hear that, Tim?"

"I'm afraid so, Marge. I think I better go back to the office and update my resume before they send the security guards to escort me out of the building. Hopefully I'll be luckier than Tom Quinn when it comes to getting some severance pay. What were you thinking, telling Mrs. Quinn to get a lawyer so she could sue the firm?"

"Oh, stop worrying" said Marge. "Even Mickey Finn

won't take a case like that on a contingency. She's got nothing in writing from BLT, and she doesn't even know what her husband was talking about when he told her there was a lot of money coming in. She might make a few calls, but nothing will come of it. In the meantime we'll solve this Simpson thing. After all, now we know that today was payday."

"Marge, maybe it really was a joke."

"Why would he be so specific about the date? There must be something about today. Was there anything in that folder they found on Quinn's desk?"

"No, nothing about a date. The only special thing about today in the Simpson case was that we were supposed to go to court to put a settlement on the record or pick a trial date. You know which one was going to happen. If it was a payday, it was Harold Simpson's payday, not Tom Quinn's."

Marge's mouth dropped open.

"Harold Simpson's payday!" Tim repeated.

Marge grabbed his arm. "Let's go."

— 32 —

TOM QUINN'S "SIMPSON" FOLDER was still on Tim's desk when
he entered his office. He took it and carried it with him as he
left the building and walked to the New York Public Library
on Fifth Avenue at Forty-Second Street, where Marge was
waiting for him. She believed it would be better if they reviewed the file away from the office and Tim agreed. Entering
the library's cavernous reading room, he saw Marge sitting
at one of the tables and went over to join her. They looked at
one another with a shared feeling of excitement, sure that the
code word "Payday" would unlock the folder's mysteries and
solve the riddle of the missing Will.

Two hours later, their excitement had turned to despair.
This time they looked at one another with frustration and
disappointment.

"Let's go through this once more, Tim."

"That shouldn't take long."

"I know, but maybe we'll notice something that hasn't
jumped out at us in the past two and a half hours."

"Okay. Let's start again with the statute," Tim exhaled.
"It says anyone can file his Will in the Surrogate's Court for

safekeeping, but it has to be in the Surrogate's Court in the county where the person lives."

"And Rex Simpson lived in Manhattan, right?"

"Right. In the co-op on the East Side."

"And that's New York County."

"Right again. The court is downtown, near City Hall on Chambers Street, in the Hall of Records."

"So maybe it was sent to Rex Simpson with the old Will and he misplaced it or dropped it or something. It sounds like he was a little at loose ends around that time. And maybe somebody found it, and was told by the cops or someone else to bring it down to the court. I know that's a stretch, but why not check it out?"

"That's an awful lot of maybes, Marge, and anyway I already told you that's where the probate proceeding is pending, so it would have shown up on the court's records when we filed the probate petition."

"Okay. Not there. So what about the paper that has a phone number written—"

Tim stopped her.

"Wait a second, Marge. I was the one who filed the probate petition. I was brand new, and I didn't know there could already be a Will there. Nobody told me anything about that, and I certainly didn't check it out. I don't even know how you would do it if you wanted to. Besides, no one at BLT would even dream about putting a Will anywhere but in the office safe. So they wouldn't look for any client's Will at the courthouse. Ken Clark actually called this statute 'the poor man's Will safe' and said it wasn't a procedure any reputable firm would utilize. But why would Tom put a copy of it in his Simpson file? Maybe we should check it out."

"I think it's worth a shot. How do we go about it?"

"I wish I knew. I guess we should go down to the court and see if one of the clerks can help us. But it's too late to go today. Five o'clock is not prime time for finding living souls at the courthouse. I'll go tomorrow or Monday and see what

I can find out."

"Good. What's next?"

Tim pointed to one of the sheets of paper. "There's this telephone number. 212-134-8212. Assuming it is a telephone number, it would be here in New York City, except for one thing. Like I said before, telephone numbers can't start with a 'one.' I don't know why, but they can't. So that looks like a dead end, but it's hard to believe someone like Tom would be so precise in writing down a number that made no sense."

"Why don't I kick that around when I get back to the office on Monday?" Marge said. "Maybe he just miswrote the first digit of the exchange. I can run 234, 334, 434, et-cetera. I've got loads of telephone books that I use to track down people like deadbeat husbands. Maybe I'll come up with something."

"Okay. Now we've got the check number. 3106."

"I know it says 'check number,' Tim, but couldn't it be a reminder to, say, check one of your firm's files with that file number?"

"We don't have a file number 3106. I already looked."

"Could it be one of the court's file numbers, like the one for the Simpson case?"

"No again, Marge. The number is different. I've seen it so many times, I know it by heart. And the sequence is wrong, anyway."

"What do you mean?"

"I've had to work on a few other estates since I've been here, and the file number for a New York County estate al-ways starts with the year of the first activity in the estate. Then there's a hyphen, and after that a number which indi-cates the estate's sequence in that year's new estate filings. So let's say a probate proceeding is filed in the John Jones Estate in 1965, and it's the two hundred seventy-fifth new estate to come into the court that year. The file number would be 1965-275. After that, any proceeding brought in that estate will have the same file number. No, I think we have to assume

3106 is a check number, just like it says."

"Do you think it could be a BLT check that was used to pay three dollars to the Surrogate's Court Clerk? If it was, then we'd know what it was for and how it was connected to Simpson. Can you find out?"

"I don't think it would go over too well with Rem if I asked him if I could take a look at BLT's check register. I guess I could ask him whether he knows what could have been the reason for a three dollar fee being paid to the court in Simpson. I mean it is something that was in Tom's Simpson folder and I think he'd understand my wanting to check it out. Maybe it ties in to the date of the 'receipt' referred to in the folder. I'll go ahead and ask Rem."

"Good. Do that, but it looks like all we're really sure about is that address written on the other piece of paper," said Marge. "Didn't Rex have another home out in the Hamptons?"

"Yes, he did. In East Hampton."

"That's a high-priced neighborhood. Why did he get to keep that and the Manhattan co-op in the divorce? Did he have a pre-nup?"

"I don't know. He also got the hunting cabin upstate. His ex-wife got their place in Palm Beach, an interest in a silver mine in Nevada, and a huge investment account they had at Chevy Chase Trust in Maryland."

"How huge?"

"Twenty million."

"That's huge. Why don't I have a few clients like that?"

"Maybe she'll come to you next time, Marge."

"Next time?"

"The talk around the office is that she's already remarried, and the new husband has a habit of taking suspicious 'business trips.' She may need a good investigator to keep an eye on him. I'll give her your name if she calls."

"I can hardly wait. In the meantime, what's this address doing in Quinn's folder?"

"I just don't know. It's about the only thing in there we're sure about, but we don't even know why it's there. And why the question mark? It's frustrating."

"Say that to me again." Marge snapped her fingers and pointed her index finger at him.

"I said it was frustrating."

"No, you said it was the only thing *in* the folder that we're sure about. What about what's *on* the folder?"

"You mean Rex Simpson's name?"

"Right. It just says, 'Simpson.' How do we know it's Rex Simpson?"

"Who else would it be?"

"How about *Harold* Simpson?"

33

"THREE DOLLARS? I never knew anything in the court could be that cheap. That's got to be a mistake."

Rem didn't promise to be much help here. "What does this have to do with wrapping up the case, anyway?"

Tim interpreted this question to mean either he was wasting his and Watson's time, which translated to the dreaded "unbillable time" in the lexicon of BLT, or worse, that he was once again demonstrating that he just didn't belong.

"Virginia, could you come in here for a second?"

Virginia Martin hustled in, brandishing a pen and holding a steno pad, poised and ready for her orders.

"Yes, Mr. Watson?"

The use of first names was apparently not a two-way street where a senior partner's personal secretary was involved.

"Virginia, would you check the disbursement record in the Simpson Estate and see what payments have been made to the Surrogate's Court? Tim wants to know if there were any for three dollars."

"Certainly, Mr. Watson. Anything else?" asked Virginia, not even putting her pen to the pad.

"Tim?" Watson turned to him.

Tim knew he was pressing his luck, but it was risk Watson's ire now or face Marge's later. "Well, if there isn't anything in the Simpson Estate, I thought it wouldn't hurt to see if there was a three dollar disbursement in one of the other files Tom was working on when he died. Maybe that would explain why he felt the payment was somehow relevant to Simpson."

"Okay, Tim, but that's it," said Rem. "I don't want the entire office to stop functioning while we all look to see where your three dollars went."

Watson resumed his perusal of the documents on his desk, signaling the end of the discussion. As Tim and Virginia left, she looked at him sympathetically, confirming his fear that he was pressing his luck with this project.

Back at his desk, Tim resumed working on the draft of the settlement stipulation that Rem wanted ready for next Thursday's conference at the Surrogate's Court. It was then that the settlement with Harold Simpson would be entered into formally and placed on the record, and Rem wanted to have a blueprint for the specifics of what he'd like to see in the agreement. He had instructed Tim to include the confidentiality clause, just in case he could persuade the court to change its position on sealing files. It was a long shot, but worth a try, even though Finley was unlikely to go for it, given his penchant for trumpeting his victories widely as triumphs of the downtrodden, meaning his clients, over those who oppressed them, meaning anyone who happened to be on the other side of a case. This would be particularly true here, where the villain was represented by one of the old line firms, whom he referred to as the "White Shoe Boys" given what he assumed was their customary footwear at their Southampton lawn parties and cricket matches.

34

LATER THAT DAY, Tim's office phone rang. He picked it up.

"Mr. O'Leary, it's Virginia Martin. I looked through the disbursement record for every file Mr. Quinn worked on during the last three years. There are no three dollar disbursements, not to the Surrogate's Court or to anyone else. Not in the Simpson matter, not in any matter. Sorry."

"Thank you for your efforts, Miss Martin," said Tim. "I do have one other question, though. Could Mr. Quinn have written a personal check for something like that and then put in a request for reimbursement? Wouldn't the disbursement be to him, then, and not to the court?"

"Yes it would, Mr. O'Leary. The lawyers do that from time to time, but it still shows as a disbursement for that client matter and it shows what was spent by the lawyer that's being reimbursed. I thought of that, so I checked. Nothing showed up in the disbursement record, either in the Simpson Estate or in any other matter Mr. Quinn was working on."

"Okay. I shouldn't have taken up your time with this, but thanks."

"No problem, Mr. O'Leary. That's what I'm here for."

Tim, suspecting that Rem Watson would not share Miss Martin's characterization of her role at the firm, hung up the phone and turned his attention back to the stipulation, but found it difficult to concentrate. There had to be something he wasn't thinking of. There had to be a reason Quinn put that note in the folder. Suddenly another thought hit him. He looked up Quinn's home number in the firm directory and dialed.

"Hello?"

"Mrs. Quinn? Sorry to bother you. It's Timothy O'Leary from Bradford, Lord and Turner."

"Oh, Mr. O'Leary. So nice of you to call. And how is that lovely young lady of yours, Margery?"

"She's fine, Mrs. Quinn, thanks. She's back in New Haven where she works, but she asked me to say hello if I spoke to you again." A little white lie now and then couldn't hurt, could it?

"Isn't that nice! I wish everyone from your office was as friendly as you two. Why, just this morning I was thinking how unfair it is to be left like this, after all Tom did for the firm. My friends can't believe it."

Kitty was getting warmed up again. When she paused to take a breath, Tim jumped in.

"I know it's so hard for you, Mrs. Quinn. I don't want to be the one to remind you of all that, but I was actually thinking of something that might help a little bit."

Mrs. Quinn was up for this kind of news.

"What would that be?" she asked with eagerness.

"Well, it's really very small, but I learned today at the office that our attorneys sometimes pay for things out of their own pockets which are then charged to the clients. You know, like gas and tolls when they have to go to court on Long Island. Meal expenses they incur during business lunches. Things like that. When they get a chance, they fill out an expense slip and submit it to the office bookkeeper, who reimburses them and allocates the expenditure to the appropriate client account. It seems as if Mr. Quinn hadn't done that in several months, so he may have some payment coming if you have the receipts."

This was not exactly the bonanza Mrs. Quinn had thought might be coming her way.

"Oh, I don't think so, Mr. O'Leary," said Mrs. Quinn, sounding deflated. "Tom wasn't the three-martini lunch type, and he wasn't the one who wined and dined clients at the Yale Club. That was the high and mighty partners' department. Why, he was lucky if one of them offered to bring back a sandwich for him, so he could keep working on their precious clients' Wills and trusts."

"I guess so, Mrs. Quinn, but just this morning I was looking at a folder he kept in the Simpson matter, and he had put a note in there about a clerk asking for a three dollar fee. He even wrote down what looks like a check number, 3106. That seems like an awfully high number for a personal check. Still, I thought I should call just to make sure. Because if it was a personal check, he should have been reimbursed, but he hadn't put in for it before he died."

"Oh, that! You know I saw that check. They don't even give you back your cancelled checks these days unless you pay a fee, but I paid it—I want those checks! Unbelievable what these banks get away with. Why, just yesterday I had to go in and complain to the branch manager—"

"Excuse me, Mrs. Quinn," Tim interrupted her, "but did you say you saw a copy of the check?" His heart raced.

Mrs. Quinn grumbled a bit at this interruption of her story.

"What check, Mr. O'Leary?"

"The one to the court for three dollars. You saw it?"

"Oh, did I ever. I balance the checkbook, you know. Tom had other things to do, and, to be honest with you, he was a little too generous with those charities, with their sob stories pleading for another contribution before your last check even clears. One of them even says if you check a box on their form that says you don't want any more solicitations from them, and send it with or without a contribution, they'll never ask you again. Hah! Think that works?"

"Mrs. Quinn, the three dollar check."

"Oh, that again. Yes, I saw it. There it was in the statement. As soon as I saw it, I said to Tom, 'Are we paying your rich clients' bills now? Isn't it hard enough just to pay our own? You make sure we get this back now.'"

"But he didn't?"

"No, he said it was personal, and to just forget about it. How do you like that? Paying somebody's court fees with our money."

His pulse still pounding, Tim tried his best to sound casual. "Do you still have a copy of the check?"

"Of course. I keep all of our financial records for six years, just like our accountant told us to do."

"Could you get it out now?"

"I suppose. If you really want me to."

"If you don't mind."

"Just a minute." Tim could hear the shuffling of papers on the other end. "It should be here in this drawer with the others. I think it was late last summer. Yes. Here it is. Three dollars, payable to 'Clerk, Surrogate's Court.' It's in the statement for last August."

"What else does it say?"

"Nothing at all. Tom didn't even fill out the memorandum line. That was so unlike him. He was usually so precise."

"Did he enter it in your check register?"

"No. That's why I was so surprised when the statement came in. I knew there was a check unaccounted for in the register, but I thought maybe it was in his wallet and he'd tell me when he used it. Can I get the firm to reimburse me for this?"

"Well, why don't you see if he had any other expenses in the last few months that should be reimbursed and then send them to me so I can see what can be done. In the meantime, could I stop by today and pick that one up? The Simpson matter is on the calendar next Thursday, and it might be good to have the check for that."

"I can't imagine what difference three dollars would make in an estate of that size, but if you really need it … It's Friday so I'm going to bridge now, but I'll be back after five if you'd like to come by then. Why don't you bring Margery with you? I'd love to see her again."

"I'm sorry, Mrs. Quinn, but as I said before, she's up where she works in Connecticut today. Maybe next time she comes down?"

"Oh, I'm getting so forgetful these days. Well, five o'clock then?"

"Five o'clock. I'll be there. See you then."

MRS. QUINN LET TIM take check number 3106, but only as far as a local copy shop, since, she reminded him, she was religious about holding on to all financial documents for the prescribed six years. Once he had made a few Xerox copies of the check, he returned to her house so he could drop off the original before he headed back to his apartment.

He found Mrs. Quinn in an unexpectedly gay mood, as she greeted him with an equally unexpected invitation. "Come inside, Mr. O'Leary. You have to meet my grandchildren. They stopped by to cheer me up. In fact, why don't you join us for dinner? I'll put a roast in the oven, and we can all get to know one another while we wait for it to be ready."

Tim wasn't too sure how long it took to cook a roast, but he suspected it might be quite awhile. He also knew Kitty's moods tended to take nosedives at fairly short time intervals, but he was curious about Tom Quinn's grandchildren, so he said he would stay for a cup of tea before heading back to Manhattan.

"A cup of tea? It's cocktail time, young man! Happy hour, as your generation likes to say. Loosen up, you're in Brooklyn now, not on Park Avenue. Now what will you have? We've always kept a well stocked bar in the Quinn household."

Mrs. Quinn hooked her arm in his and steered him toward an adjacent room where the grandchildren were sitting on a couch, suppressing grins as their grandmother approached. Happy hour was apparently not a time when mood swings would be a problem.

"Mr. O'Leary, these are my beautiful grandchildren, Kevin and Megan. Children, this is Timothy O'Leary from grandpa's office."

They stood and shook hands with him.

"Please call me Tim," he said. "And I wish you would call me Tim also, Mrs. Quinn."

"Well fine, Tim. And of course, I'm Kitty."

With the introductions out of the way, Kitty instructed them all to sit while she made drinks for herself and Tim. Kevin and Megan already had Cokes in front of them, as befitted their age, at least when grandma was around.

"What will you have, Tim?"

"Whatever you're having, Kitty," he replied, hoping she wouldn't come back with a chocolate mango liqueur.

"Don't be silly. You should have what you like. As I said, we've always kept a well-stocked bar for our guests."

"Do you have beer? Or red wine?"

"Domestic or imported?"

"You mean the beer?"

"Either." The evening was proving to be full of surprises.

"How about the beer?"

"Well, for imported we have Heineken, Stella, Becks light and dark, St. Pauli Girl, Guinness and Killian's Irish Red— that was Tom's favorite—and then for American beer ... What are you giggling about, you two?"

"What do you have on tap, Grandma?" They were both laughing now, and Tim was on the verge himself. Rather than having his host recite her selection of domestic beers and the contents of what he suspected might rival the finest wine cellars in Manhattan, he took advantage of the momentary distraction to announce his selection.

"I'll have Tom's favorite, Kitty. Killian's Irish Red would be great."

"Are you sure, Tim? Don't pay attention to these two. They're just trying to tease their old Grandma. Maybe you'd prefer a highball?"

"A highball?"

"You know, a mixed drink. Rye and ginger. Rum and coke. Scotch and soda. Or a glass of port or sherry? I can tell you what we have."

"No, no. Please, Kitty. Killian's will be perfect."

After Kitty fetched his beer, she returned to the bar and, a few minutes later, came back with a large martini glass. Rather than containing a standard martini's components—clear gin and vermouth, and perhaps an olive on a toothpick—Kitty's glass was filled with a bright-blue liquid resembling Windex, in which a lemon peel was immersed.

"What's that, Kitty?" The sight of it made Tim purse his lips.

"Oh, it's a blue martini," she said. "White vermouth, blue curacao, and a healthy dose of gin. Makes me feel warm and fuzzy inside," she winked.

"Are you sure it isn't windshield wiper fluid, Grandma?" asked Kevin. He and Megan broke into laughter again, Kitty shushing them.

After that, the four of them settled into a surprisingly comfortable conversation. Tim learned that the grandchildren lived nearby in the neighborhood. Megan was active on her school paper and in the drama club, and Kevin played guitar in a folk group with friends. Kitty boasted that she'd seen both of them perform, although the drama club's shows were "a little easier on the ears" than Kevin's band. Happy Hour was clearly Kitty's favorite time of the day, and having her grandchildren with her only added to her good spirits. A second round of drinks was served, and the cooking aromas emanating from the kitchen were becoming irresistible. The pleasant conversation continued. Inevitably, when bright young teenagers are present, an adult will inquire about their plans for the future and about what college they hope to attend. Tim did so.

Suddenly, the bonhomie evaporated, and a somber Megan answered for herself and her brother.

"I was accepted at Georgetown, but it looks like I won't be able to go. Grandpa had said he'd pay for it. He was really excited about me going there, but now that he's gone, Grandma just can't afford it, and Mom has no money."

Tim put his beer down on the table, remembering too late what Kitty had said at the wake.

"I'm going to have to get a job to help out at home, at least for now," Megan continued. "I'll try to take courses at Kingsborough Community when I can."

Kitty let out a whimper.

"Kevin and I both have good grades. I think he would have gotten into Notre Dame next year, but it looks like that's not in the cards for him either," said Megan, not slowing down. Tim could see this was an emotional issue for her and regretted his mistake in bringing up the subject. Kevin stared self-consciously at his soda.

"Actually, he might have to drop out of Xaverian High and do his senior year at the public high school," she went on. "I'm lucky, I guess, since Grandpa had already paid my tuition for Fontbonne Hall this year, so I'll at least be able to graduate from there this June."

"That's a shame, Megan," said Tim. "I'm surprised those colleges don't have scholarships for situations like yours."

"They do. But they don't cover everything, and there would still be more left over than we could afford to pay, even if we took jobs on campus."

"What about student loans?"

"We don't qualify, at least not for how much we would need. Mom went through a bankruptcy two years ago, so no one will lend to her, and we can't get enough on our own. Even if we could, who knows if we'd even be able to pay it off after college?"

Tim noticed Mrs. Quinn was weeping quietly over her third blue martini, but this time he couldn't blame her. Then he had an idea.

"Wait a minute! Didn't your dad die in Egypt during the Suez Crisis in '57? Was he part of the UN peacekeeping mission? There must be veteran's benefits for things like his children's college expenses."

"Oh, that. Grandma always tells people Dad died in Egypt during the Suez Crisis. What she doesn't mention was that he died from a heart attack on a Mediterranean cruise he and my mother won in a church raffle. Actually, they never got to Egypt because the cruise ship turned around when all the trouble started. He wasn't in the service. We didn't have troops there, anyway. I learned that in World History."

She stopped. "We've been having such a nice time tonight. Let's not ruin it with this," she said.

"You're right, Megan," said Tim, relieved. "Let's change the subject, but don't give up hope. You and your brother are obviously very smart and talented. Something will work out, I'm sure. In the meantime, Kitty, that roast smells great. If you don't mind, I'll stay for dinner after all."

The tone turned back to a happier one for the rest of the evening, and Tim enjoyed himself. Still, it gnawed at him that he wanted to help these two kids, yet didn't know how.

36

"WHERE WERE YOU last night? I tried to call."

Tim wasn't sure whether Marge sounded concerned or suspicious.

"I was at your friend Kitty Quinn's house, Marge. I spent a very nice evening with her and her two grandchildren, Kevin and Megan. We had drinks, and I stayed for dinner. They were really great kids. I know you'd like them, but it's sort of sad. Tom Quinn was going to put them through college, but now they can't go. No money. And—"

"Whoa, Tim. Slow down a minute. What were you doing there in the first place? I thought we were going to check in with one another about the Simpson case. We're running out of time, you know."

"That's why I was there. Rem's secretary looked through our office records yesterday. There's no indication of any three dollar check having been drawn by the firm to the Clerk of the Surrogate's Court for the Simpson case, or for any of the estates Tom himself was handling. And Tom never put in for reimbursement for any payment he might have made from his own funds for a client."

"Maybe he wrote a check for something and just hadn't gotten around to asking for reimbursement when he died."

"Bingo! That's what I thought. So I called your friend Kitty."

"Tim, would you stop calling her my friend Kitty? I got along with her, but really."

"Marge, I call her Kitty now, too. She asked me to. Maybe I should say 'our friend Kitty.'"

"Just get to the point, please. What were you doing at her house?"

"That's what I'm trying to tell you. I called to see if she knew about any check her husband might have written to the Surrogate's Court for three dollars, and sure enough, she did! Tom wrote a check in that amount on August 7, 1968, but he wouldn't tell her what it was for. She was really annoyed. Anyway, I asked if I could make a copy of the cancelled check and she said okay. I went down there around five yesterday, got the check and took it to a local copy shop to make a few copies for us. She still wanted the original, so I brought it back to her at the house, and there were the grandkids. Next thing you know, we were having cocktails and then dinner. They're really nice kids." Tim stopped to take a breath.

"Wow! You're starting to sound like a detective yourself, Tim. If you ever decide you're tired of working for the big bucks in your Park Avenue digs, maybe I can use you in my shop."

"You pay the going rate?"

"Absolutely. Assuming you mean two dollars per hour to start, with a dollar raise when you get your gun license."

"You carry a gun?"

"No, but doesn't everyone down there in New York?"

"Only the cops and the schoolteachers. Thanks for the offer, but I'll have to think it over."

"Seriously, Tim, it sounds like you actually found something that ties into that folder of Quinn's. But what does it mean? Was the check made out to the Surrogate's Court?"

"Yes, 'Clerk, Surrogate's Court,' to be exact. There has to be some connection to the Simpson case, but I just don't know what it is. I thought it might have something to do with that statute that was in the folder, but I looked at it again and the fee for filing a Will in Surrogate's Court for safekeeping is five dollars, not three dollars. The statute says the fee can be reduced or waived, so I'm going down to the courthouse on Monday morning to see whether they ever charge a lower fee and, if so, whether the Simpson Will might actually have been filed there."

"Why would Quinn do that?"

"I have no idea. But I think it's worth checking out."

37

"HOW DID IT GO?" Tim had called Marge on returning from his Monday morning visit to the Surrogate's Court.

"Not so well, I'm afraid. First, the clerk told me, 'Number one, we don't give discounts. Haven't you heard about the fiscal crisis?'"

"What fiscal crisis?"

"He didn't say. What he did say was, 'Didn't you check for a Will before you filed the petition?' But I think he just said that so I would feel stupid—as if I didn't already—because before I could answer he said that they would have run a check for Rex Simpson's Will in their records before they accepted the probate petition. He told me sometimes he wonders if attorneys 'from these big firms even bother to read the papers before they file them. After all,' he said, 'the form for the petition clearly states you've reviewed the court's files and there is nothing on file relating to this decedent.' Bottom line, to use his words, 'The Simpson Will is not on file in the New York County Surrogate's Court, young man.'"

"It was a good idea to check anyway, Tim. I'm afraid I didn't have much better luck with the phone number. None of the permutations led me anywhere. One was really weird, though. If you reverse (212) 134-8212, you get (212) 843-1212, another New York City number but in an exchange out in Queens County. I figured it was worth a try, but when I dialed the number, the person who answered told me it was a Catholic Church, Our Lady of Perpetual Help in someplace called South Ozone Park. I excused myself and hung up."

"Did you say Ozone Park, Marge?"

"No. South Ozone Park."

"Marge, I think that's where Harold Simpson lives."

"You're kidding!"

"No, although we can safely assume Harold is not a priest. Do you think if you reshuffled the last four digits of that telephone number, it might be his home phone?"

"I can do better than that. I can just look up Harold's name in the phone book. Wait a minute, I'm doing it right now. Damn!"

"What's the matter, Marge?"

"Nothing listed," she said. "Would you have a number for him in your office's file?"

"I'll check and get back to you, but I doubt it. We'd have no reason to contact him while his brother was alive, and we're not allowed to speak to him now. He's a person on the other side of a litigation who has his own lawyer. The only possibility would be if someone in the office tried to call him after Rex died to see whether he'd sign a consent to the probate of the Will. Considering that it disinherited him, I don't think anyone would even try. Tom Quinn said as much when he was helping me with the probate papers."

"Okay, I'll call a couple of investigators I know. Maybe they'll have some ideas. Let's talk later today."

Marge hung up, and Tim piled the now-bulky Simpson Estate files onto his desk. He looked without success for Harold Simpson's contact information, but something else turned up which surprised him. Rex had used his East Hampton address on his personal income tax returns. Tim called Rem to see if he should change the address he had been using on the draft of the stipulation of settlement.

"That rascal." Rem seemed amused. "I guess old Rex didn't like paying New York City income taxes. We don't prepare clients' income tax returns, but he must have told his accountant to use that address. I'd love to know when was the last time he even slept in that place. His ex used to stay out there when she was in town, so he gave it a wide berth during the final years of their marriage. I always thought it was ironic that he wound up with it in the divorce, but she wanted the Palm Beach place and said East Hampton had become 'boring.' That was after the local police enforced an ordinance that imposed a 3 a.m. curfew on the type of high-decibel rock music she featured at her all night pool parties.

"Anyway, even after the divorce, Rex still didn't use it very much as far as I could tell. So don't worry about it, Tim. Keep using the Manhattan address. That's where he lived."

38

MARGE HAD NO LUCK shuffling the numbers, and concluded that it probably wasn't even a telephone number at all. Before abandoning the idea completely, though, she tried one more call to the church.

"Our Lady of Perpetual Help. Victor speaking. How may I help you?" The person who answered sounded young and cheerful, obviously not Harold Simpson assuming an alias.

"I'm sorry to bother you. I know you're probably busy, but my name is Margery Conley. I'm a private investigator working for an attorney who is involved in a Will contest in the Manhattan Surrogate's Court."

"Uh, okay," said Victor.

"A telephone number found in the client file seems to be the exact reverse of your church's number, and since the number makes no sense when we read it forward—there's a 'one' after the area code—I just thought the person who wrote it down might have reversed it intentionally for some reason. Anyway, I know it's a long shot, but that's why I'm calling. To see if there's any connection."

"Connection?"

"Yes. You know, to the case."

"What case?"

"Oh, I'm sorry. The case in the Surrogate's Court. The one about the Will. It's called the Simpson case."

"I think you should probably speak to Sister Jeanne. I'm just an eighth grader. I answer the phone on Mondays during lunch hour, so Mrs. Daugherty can go out to lunch. Most of the people who call want to know what time Masses are scheduled, or when Father Michael hears confessions. Stuff like that. I don't really know about cases or courts."

"Oh, I'm so sorry." Marge realized this was the third time she had said she was sorry in about a minute or less. She guessed it was a Catholic thing, from her own parochial school days.

"Of course, Victor," she sighed. "I'd be happy to speak to Sister Jeanne. Is she there?"

"No. She went to lunch with Mrs. Daugherty."

"Could you give her a message for me? Could you ask her to call me? I'll give you my number."

Victor was back on familiar territory. The message having been dutifully recorded, he hung up and resumed eating his sandwich. Kids had to eat lunch too.

An hour later, Marge's phone rang. It was Sister Jeanne.

"Victor told me you called about a Will. Is the church a beneficiary?" she asked, almost breathless with excitement. "That would be so wonderful! We do our best to keep costs down, but the people here in Ozone Park simply have too little money to support a church and a school and their families at the same time."

She was speaking rapidly now, not leaving any opening for Marge to interrupt her flow.

"And Victor said you told him there was a number for us, but he couldn't remember what it was. Oh, I'm getting way ahead of myself. I'm sorry."

The Catholic thing again.

"Sister Jeanne, I'm so sorry." And again! "I'm afraid I

explained things in a way that Victor must have found very confusing. It looks like he got your hopes up and I'm going to have to disappoint you."

"There's no legacy for OLPH?"

"OLPH?"

"Our Lady of Perpetual Help."

"Unfortunately, no. Sister, there's a case pending in court about the Will of a man who died in Manhattan. What looks like a phone number was written on a piece of paper in one of the law firm's files, but the number makes no sense unless you read it backwards, and then it becomes the number of your church. One of the lawyers and I thought that maybe there was some connection between Our Lady of Perpetual Help and the decedent. I know we're grasping at straws, but I thought I should call just in case."

"Well, we'd be happy to help if we can. I'm sorry I sounded so greedy before. It's been difficult lately, what with the economy and so many of our old parishioners moving away. What would you like to know?"

"Have you ever heard the name Reginald Simpson?"

"Reginald? I don't think so."

"His nickname was Rex."

"I'm sorry, but I'm afraid we don't have any Reginalds or Rexes here. We have Roccos and Rosarios and Rashans and Rositas and names like that. About the only Simpson I know is Harold, and he's still alive as far as I know."

Margery gasped.

"Are you all right, dear?"

"Yes, Sister, I'm fine. Did you say Harold Simpson?"

"Why yes, dear. Harold lives around here and he comes by now and then. He doesn't attend Mass frequently, but he likes to visit the church and say a few prayers before he goes over to the race track. He says it brings him luck. 'Better than a rabbit's foot,' he says. We don't encourage that approach to our faith, of course, but at least it shows some awareness of the power of the Almighty. Anyway, that's neither here nor there, is it? Harold is obviously not who you're interested in."

"Sister Jeanne, I may be very interested in him. He might actually be related to Reginald Simpson, the man who died. But that still doesn't explain why your number would be in the file, if that really was supposed to be your number, in reverse. You see, the person who wrote the number down was one of the attorneys in the law firm I mentioned when I called and spoke to your Victor earlier. But that lawyer died suddenly a little over a week ago, and we only came across the number after he passed away. Do you have any idea why your number would have been in the file?"

"Well certainly, dear. Harold doesn't have a telephone, so sometimes he gives people our number. When they call we take messages for him. He stops by now and then to see if anyone has called for him."

"Do you do that for a lot of people?"

"A few. It's a way we can help. And many of them try to reciprocate when they can. Not so much with money, which they really can't spare, but maybe by bringing flowers from their garden for the church's altar, or helping clean the school rooms. Things like that. Harold is a little different."

"How so?"

"If he has a good day over at the racetrack, he stops by and gives us a little share of the money. He told me last week that he's got a 'sure thing' coming up this week and he's going to 'cut us in for a piece of the action,' but I don't take that too seriously. There have been too many hearts broken by 'sure things' in this parish since I've been here. Aqueduct Raceway is practically right around the corner, you know."

"Sister Jeanne, does your Harold Simpson live on 118th Street?"

"Why yes he does, dear. At least I think so. He's never officially registered as a parishioner here, but I think he did once say that was where he lived. Lately he's been saying that he's going to move, as soon as his 'big score' comes in. 'Big score,' that's another expression he's been using lately."

Marge could hardly breathe.

"Sister, believe it or not, Reginald Simpson actually had a brother named Harold. I think it may be the same person you're talking about. Do you know if he's received any phone calls about the Reginald Simpson Estate?"

"Well, I don't know anything about that. He hasn't had very many callers, at least until several months ago, when he did started getting a number of calls from a Mr. Quinn."

39

THE PHONE on Tim's desk rang.

"Tim, I think we've got something!" It was Marge. "Tom Quinn was calling Harold Simpson. That telephone number was the church's number, I guess written backwards in case anyone came across it. Quinn would call there when he wanted to reach Harold. Whoever answered the phone would take the message and leave it for Harold the next time he stopped by. He didn't have a phone of his own, so he told people that's how he could be reached."

"Holy shit, Marge. Tom could have gotten disbarred for that. We're not allowed to talk to another lawyer's client in the middle of a litigation. What were the messages?"

"There weren't any. Quinn would just ask whoever took the call to have Harold call him."

"At BLT?"

"No. It was a different number. I've already checked it out. It was a private phone number belonging to T. Quinn at the Brooklyn address. He must have kept the phone in his home office. Maybe in a desk drawer with the ringer off when he wasn't home. Who knows?"

"My God. Did Finley call Harold at the church also?"

"Yes. But he left his office number, at least in the beginning. After that, he'd just say something like 'he knows my number,' and tell Sister Jeanne to 'tell that pain in the ass to get himself a telephone like everyone else in the world.' I was a little surprised when she repeated it verbatim."

"Did Finley make reference to Quinn, or vice versa?"

"No. Quinn would just politely leave his name and number, and Finley would just as impolitely leave his."

"Did it sound like their calls were connected, at least from a time standpoint?"

"No, not even that."

"So where do we go from here, Marge? We've already deposed Harold at length. Finley will never let us have another crack at him. We've certified to the judge that pretrial discovery is complete, so I doubt he'd order him back. It wouldn't make any difference anyway. Harold wouldn't tell the truth about the calls. And we can't talk to Tom, unless we can line up a medium to conduct a séance."

"I don't have any mediums on my Rolodex, Tim."

"Oh boy, I don't know how Rem is going to react when I tell him, which I think I have to. He may have to tell the court about Tom's communications with Harold, and at the very least it will be embarrassing to the firm. My God, what have we gotten ourselves into?"

"I don't know, Tim, but we can't sit on our hands. Tom Quinn took that Will. I'm sure of it. And that creep Harold must have been involved somehow. Now he's going to get thirty million dollars, and everyone else—Teddy Bracken, Quinn's grandchildren, and your firm—is going to get screwed. We've got to do something! We've got to think of something."

"Marge, even assuming Quinn took the Will, and I grant you he probably did, there's no way to find it now. If he gave it to Harold, it's been destroyed. Harold would have been sure of that."

"But Quinn was getting something in return, his 'big pay-day,'" said Marge. "Quinn knew what Rex thought of his brother. There's no way he would have just trusted Harold to pay him when the time came. You can't put this type of bargain in writing, so how could he be sure that Harold would pay? There's one way and one way only. Harold had to know the Will still existed, and that if he didn't share the money with Quinn, it would be produced."

"Okay, Marge, let's say you're right. Let's say the Will still exists. Where would it be? Kitty Quinn told me she was getting ready to probate Tom's Will. BLT is going to do it for her gratis, but she has to get his financial records together first. And when she was retelling her tale of financial woe, she mentioned that she had reviewed all of Tom's private papers and opened all of his safe deposit boxes. There were no surprises, much less a Will signed by Rex Simpson. Of course the main thrust of her description of the search focused on the financial side. Her exact words on that subject were, 'Tom didn't leave me enough to get me up one aisle at the supermarket.' Just to be certain, I asked her if there were any important business papers like Wills in Tom's files or in the safe deposit boxes, and she sarcastically asked if that would include Tom's meritorious service certificate from the Knights of Columbus and his high roller award from the Hibernian Society's winter bowling league."

"But Tim, he wouldn't have given the Will to Harold. I know he wouldn't. So where is it? And why wasn't it in the folder on his desk? Maybe it was there, and Quinn took it out and put it somewhere else for fear that someone in the office might see it. Somewhere safe, but somewhere he could get at if Harold reneged on his end of the bargain."

Tim thought this made sense, but it still left them without any plausible solution to their problem. He said goodbye and headed for Rem Watson's office, cringing at the thought of telling him about Quinn's contacts with Harold Simpson and the possibility that Quinn had stolen the Will.

40

"HE WHAT?" Rem wasn't happy. He had already left for the day when Tim went to his office on Monday afternoon, so he had to wait until Tuesday morning to give him the news.

"He made a number of calls to Harold Simpson after Rex died. Harold didn't have a telephone so Tom left messages for him at a church in South Ozone Park, near where Harold lives. And, incidentally, near Aqueduct Racetrack where Harold apparently spent a lot of his spare time."

"Harold has nothing *but* spare time, Tim. I have a hard time imagining him inside of a church, though."

Rem sighed and leaned back in his chair. "Are you sure about this? I have no intention of telling the surrogate about it on Thursday unless you're absolutely certain. Tom Quinn may not have been a partner, but he was a well-respected part of this firm, and was known as such in the legal community. I am not going to damage his reputation, to say nothing of ours, by putting something this offensive on the record if there is any question about its accuracy."

Tim had anticipated this would be Rem's reaction, but felt he had no option other than to press on.

"I'm sorry, Rem, but the nun at Our Lady of Perpetual Help was very convincing. She even said that Harold would give the church some of his winnings from time to time when he got lucky at the track. He told her he had come across a sure thing that was going to result in a big payoff for him pretty soon, and that he would be giving the parish a chunk of it when it came in. It sounds like she took this with a grain of salt, but nevertheless that's what he said. The connection to the settlement in the probate contest is obvious, but of course she didn't know anything about that."

Watson raised an eyebrow.

"And still doesn't," Tim added hastily. "Oh, and she said Michael Finley had left a few messages for Harold as well, but she didn't think too much of him."

"Who does? All right, Tim, this was obviously very un-ethical behavior on Tom's part, but maybe it was his mis-guided way of trying to persuade Harold to do the right thing and honor his brother Rex's intentions. You know, withdraw his objections to the Will. After all, Tom was a model of legal probity. He clearly forgot himself here, but I can't imagine it was with venal intention."

Tim wasn't 100 percent sure what models of legal probity and absences of venal intentions meant, but he doubted they applied in this situation. He continued, undaunted.

"Rem, it's difficult to say this." He took a breath. "Marge and I think Tom stole the Will and was hiding it somewhere. We think he struck some kind of a bargain with Harold. To get a piece of the settlement that he knew would have to be worked out if the Will couldn't be found, and a believable argument could be made that the Will had been in Rex's pos-session before he died. We—"

"Marge? Who is Marge?"

Tim cringed. It occurred to him, for the first time, that the firm might not like outsiders checking out their cases.

"She's a friend of mine," he said, unable to silence the inner voice telling him that his career at BLT was now officially toast. "A private investigator from Connecticut. We've been talking about the case from time to time. She called the church, sort of on a whim. She didn't tell me she was going to. I'm sorry. I guess I shouldn't have done that?"

"You certainly should not have! Lord knows how many client confidences you've breached. Tom Quinn off the reservation, and now a junior associate, a *very* junior associate, decides to bring outside investigators into one of our client's matters without authorization. Young man, you and I are going to have a very serious discussion when this case is over."

Game, set, match. Tim resigned himself to looking around for a new job on Friday, but felt that in the meantime he might as well finish his report.

"Tom also used a personal check to pay the three dollars to the Surrogate's Court clerk. That was the three dollar fee I asked you about last week."

"Paid three dollars for what?"

"I don't know, Rem. I thought it might have something to do with that statute in his folder that provided for the deposit of original Wills in the Surrogate's Court for safekeeping, but another section of the same law says there's a five dollar filing fee for doing that. It also says the court can waive or reduce it, but I checked with Manhattan Surrogate's Court and they said it's five dollars, period. No reductions. And the Simpson Will wasn't there anyway. They checked when the probate petition was filed, so I have no idea what Tom's check was for."

"Nor do I, Tim, nor do I. What I do know is that this whole case is a nightmare, and it may get worse when I tell the court on Thursday about Tom's calls to Harold Simpson. What in the world was he thinking, anyway? And what were you thinking when you brought an outside investigator in on the case without getting my approval first?"

Tim shifted in his seat.

"All right, enough of this for now," said Rem. "But I want you to burn the midnight oil here. Research the question of what sanctions can be imposed on Tom Quinn's employers, namely my partners and me, for his direct contacts with a represented party in a litigated matter. I'll need that information for court Thursday. I'll see you then."

41

IT WAS PAST ELEVEN on Wednesday night when Tim returned home and slumped down into one of the old and threadbare easy chairs in the living room of his small apartment. His research hadn't turned up much, since it didn't look like whatever contacts Quinn had with Harold Simpson had worked to Harold's disadvantage. Quite the opposite, in fact, if, as Tim and Marge now believed, it was Quinn himself who made off with the Will after making some kind of arrangement with Harold, that would be to their mutual benefit.

Not that Harold's complicity, which was obvious to Tim, would deter Mickey Finley from dreaming up a scenario that would somehow make Harold the victim. Tim could see Finley arguing that Harold had been improperly influenced by Quinn to accept a settlement that was far less than his airtight case deserved. Tim was also quite sure that Harold would oblige with a version of his conversations with Quinn that would fully support this theory.

Equally problematic was the very real possibility that Quinn's actions would result in the court's referral of the matter to the Appellate Division, for a determination of whether

Bradford, Lord and Turner should be censured for the ethical violations of its now-deceased senior estates associate. Even Tim, with his total lack of experience in this area, suspected that the firm would not be held responsible for Quinn's actions by the Appellate Division. But he also knew that word of the inquiry might leak to the press, notwithstanding the supposedly confidential nature of such investigations. The partners would be mortified, and clients would head for the exits. Although he assumed his days at the firm were numbered in any event, he didn't think his involvement in a scandal-ridden litigation would enhance his job prospects anywhere else. He closed his eyes and tried to imagine life as an assistant private investigator in the firm of Margery Conley, P. I. Starting to drift off to sleep, he suddenly realized what they had been missing. He picked up the phone.

"Marge, it's me."

"Tim? You woke me up. Where are you? Is everything all right? It's after midnight."

"Marge, I need your help. I think I may know what happened to Rex Simpson's Will. The case is on tomorrow, and the you-know-what is going to hit the fan. Rem is going to tell the court about Tom's contacts with Harold Simpson, and Finley will probably act outraged and jack up his settlement demand. I'll be unemployed—and unemployable—before we're even out the courthouse door."

"Whoa, Tim, whoa. Slow down. Why would you get fired for what Quinn did?"

"Because I brought an outside investigator, you, in on the case without getting the firm's permission first. Rem was furious when he heard about it. He said we would have to have 'a very serious discussion' after the case is over."

"Oh, great. I don't know what to say. I guess I should have stayed out of this. I'm so sorry."

"Well I'm afraid I'm going to have to ask you to get back into it. To do one more thing for me."

"But Tim, you just said—"

"I know, Marge, but if I'm going to get fired anyway, I might as well take one more shot at solving this thing. If not for myself, then for Teddy Bracken. Do you remember that East Hampton address?"

"I do. It was one of Rex Watson's homes, right? The one he never used."

"That's it, but it was also the address he used on his tax returns, so he could avoid paying New York City income taxes."

"So he was a tax cheat. What does that have to do with his Will?"

"What if Quinn used that address to file the Will in Suffolk County Surrogate's Court? Remember the three dollar check to the Surrogate's Court? That could have been for the filing fee."

"But you said the filing fee was five dollars, remember?"

"Right. But keep in mind, another section of the same statute says the court can reduce the five dollar fee, or even waive it. The clerk in Manhattan acted like I was off my rocker to even suggest that a court would do such a thing, but maybe he doesn't speak for all the Surrogate's Courts—Suffolk County, in particular. So here's what I want you to do."

42

REM WATSON, GREG TROUT AND TEDDY BRACKEN were standing outside the door to the courtroom when Tim arrived. No one looked happy, and Bracken looked like he was ready to faint. They exchanged perfunctory "Good mornings," but only Trout seemed to mean it. After all, Morgan Guaranty would still receive a hefty commission, regardless of who prevailed in the probate contest. Watson asked the others to excuse him for a moment while he talked to Tim.

"What did your research show?" he asked tersely.

Tim briefly considered mentioning his new theory regarding the entries in the Quinn folder, to see if Rem could gain some time for Marge to check it out, but quickly decided that Marge's continued involvement would trigger a negative reaction at best, and quite possibly an order to call her off.

"It's pretty much what you figured, Rem. Tom's communications with Harold, while Harold was represented by counsel in the litigation that was presumably the subject matter of the contacts, was a clear violation of the Canons of Ethics, and would also be a violation of the ABA's new Model Code of Professional Responsibility. It's also clear that

Bradford, Lord and Turner, as a firm, can be held responsible for Tom's actions and subjected to disciplinary measures such as censure. Unless the firm can show that he was a 'loose cannon' acting without the firm's knowledge, and in contravention of its stated policies governing the actions of its partners and associates. That would have to be established by the firm in whatever disciplinary proceedings are initiated. An inquiry seems inevitable once the court is apprised of what happened."

"Shit! This gets worse and worse. And I suppose I have to tell the court?"

"You do. That's also in the Canons and the Code. It applies when you learn that another lawyer has committed a violation of the Rules that raises a substantial question as to the other lawyer's honesty, trustworthiness or fitness as a lawyer. Although it's obviously a little unusual for this type of thing to be discovered only after the fellow attorney dies, there's no exception mentioned for a situation like this. I can't see how Tom's death prior to our learning of what happened lessens our burden."

"Unfortunately I have to agree with you on that, Tim. I guess I'll have to tell the judge. All right, let's get back to our friends."

As they walked back to where Bracken, still looking ashen, and Trout were standing, Tim saw Harold, wearing his seemingly permanent smirk, and Finley, strutting and looking fierce, as they approached from the other direction. Business as usual.

Watson took a deep breath and waited for Finley. Tim stood at his side.

"Good morning, Michael. May I have a word with you privately before we go inside?"

"Morning, Watson. Sure, but we're not giving another inch. Your guy is lucky to be getting anything. Not another inch, you understand?"

"It's not that at all. Let's talk over here, away from the

clients." Watson motioned Finley toward the arcade that overlooked the stairway below.

Tim watched from a safe distance, knowing fireworks were about to erupt. In a moment, both men's voices could be heard loud and clear.

"He called my guy on the phone? Are you kidding? Is this how you guys operate?"

"No, no, Michael, I told you. This was totally without my knowledge. Or anyone else at the firm. I only learned about it on Tuesday. We're all horrified by it. I'm going to inform the court this morning, but I thought you deserved the courtesy of being told first."

"I have to speak to my client about this!" shouted Finley, walking over to Harold.

Tim was somewhat relieved to see that Finley was not involved in Quinn's project, given his obvious surprise on hearing the news from Rem. Nevertheless, Tim had no doubt that Finley was already calculating how this new development could work to Harold's financial advantage, and to his own.

He rejoined Watson and they went back to where Trout and Bracken were standing.

"What's the problem, Rem? What was Finley so exercised about?"

"It's a long story, Greg. Let's go inside. I'll tell you later, but I think they'll be calling the calendar in a few minutes."

— 43 —

ON THIS MORNING, the courtroom was moderately filled, primarily with attorneys, along with a sprinkling of clients. Conversations were relatively muted, as most of the socializing and bartering had been done in the hallway outside. Members of the court's law department, including Jack Zaggert, entered the courtroom and positioned themselves near where the surrogate would be sitting. Other court personnel drifted in as everyone found a seat. The calendar was about to be called. Tim nervously looked at his watch and wondered what was happening with Marge.

"All rise!" The court attendant shouted as the judge entered and took his seat at the bench. "The Surrogate's Court is now in session!"

The nameplate in front of the judge identified him as S. Samuel DiMalco. He seemed to be in a reasonably amiable frame of mind as he asked the court attendant to begin the calling of the calendar, which proceeded rapidly for several minutes until the Simpson case was called.

"Reginald Simpson!" The court attendant's voice cut through the room as Rem stood.

"For the petitioner, your honor."

From the other side of the courtroom, the raspy voice of Mickey Finley boomed. "For the objectant and rightful heir, your honor!"

The judge, apparently amused by Finley's bombast, smiled briefly and addressed them.

"Please come forward, gentlemen, and state your appearances for the record. And Mr. Finley, it will be sufficient to describe yourself as attorney for your client without rendering an opinion as to his exalted status."

Finley and Watson approached the bench, with Tim following. He checked his watch.

"Young man, do you have another appointment? Are we moving too slowly for you?" Judge DiMalco was looking at Tim, who tried, but failed, to formulate a response as a quiet chorus of laughter arose from the appreciative audience of attorneys in the courtroom. A quick glance from Rem made it quite clear that he failed to see the humor in the situation. Another nail in the coffin.

"Sorry, your honor. I thought I felt my watch vibrate and I was afraid the alarm was about to go off. I apologize, your honor." A little white lie. Perjury? Tim would have to research that one some day.

"Well, I'm glad to hear someone needs an alarm to wake him at 10 a.m. Oh, to be young again!"

More laughter from the seats.

"All right, gentlemen," said the judge, returning to business. "This matter is on for scheduling a trial date this morning, but Mr. Zaggert tells me you have reached a settlement?"

"Your honor, we have," said Rem. "But a matter has come up which I feel I must address first, preferably in chambers."

"All right, Mr. Watson. I'm sure it's important, but so is the court's calendar. Why don't you and Mr. Finley and your young, well-rested associate go with Mr. Zaggert and let him know what's on your mind? If he decides that I should see you, we can do that at the end of the calendar. Thank you, gentlemen."

Rem and Finley, followed sheepishly by Tim, turned and motioned to their respective clients to stay where they were, and then followed Jack Zaggert to his office.

Finley had not said a word.

44

"THE DEAL IS OFF."

"What do you mean, Mr. Finley? I thought Mr. Watson just told the surrogate that the settlement was still on."

"Yes, Michael, what are you talking about? And can't it wait until I've told Mr. Zaggert about the other situation?"

"Why bother? I'll save you the trouble. Listen, Jack. What Watson here wants to tell you is that one of his people, may the scoundrel rest in peace, was threatening to file some trumped up welfare fraud charges against my client if he didn't agree to settle this case on the cheap."

"On the cheap?" Zaggert asked. "Isn't this case settling for thirty million dollars? And who is the scoundrel you're referring to? Mr. Watson, what's this all about?"

"Mr. Zaggert," Rem replied. "If I may. The story Mr. Finley seems to be telling is not something I've ever heard, so I think he will have to explain that one to all of us. I can only tell you what I know."

Watson proceeded to describe the apparent contacts with Harold Simpson by a lawyer in his office, acknowledging the ethical implications but stressing that he had learned of the matter only two days earlier. He apologized on behalf of the firm and promised an internal investigation, but expressed doubt that anyone else was involved.

Finley insisted on his version of the contacts, saying he had sweated it out of his client in the very few minutes available to him after he learned about the situation that morning. He said Harold might have received some welfare benefits and unemployment compensation three years ago when he was actually working, but that Watson's guy had lied to Harold about there being a lengthy prison sentence awaiting him if his actions were reported to the authorities.

Zaggert finally interrupted.

"I think you need to speak to the judge. Let me see if he's still on the bench. I'll be right back."

When the door closed, Watson turned to Finley with an incredulous expression on his face.

"Harold told you all that?"

"Well most of it. I didn't have time to sort out all the details, but that was the gist of what he said."

"And you think thirty million is some kind of a bargain?"

"Look, Watson, you've got no case and you know it. No Will, no case, so why shouldn't Harold get ninety percent, especially with what went on here?" Finley seemed almost sincere, but of course opportunistic was not out of the question. Watson shook his head and fell silent.

"The judge will see you now." Zaggert was back. "Please come with me. He wants to see you in chambers."

They joined him and walked down the hall to the door marked with the surrogate's name. Inside they encountered a woman seated behind a desk in a small anteroom, who waved them into the judge's private office, which adjoined the courtroom through an interior door. Judge DiMalco was sitting behind his much more impressive desk and did not rise as he told them to take seats.

"Jack tells me that there's been inappropriate contact between a member of Mr. Watson's firm and Mr. Finley's client.

Is that true, Mr. Watson?"

"Yes, your honor, but it was one of our associates. Not one of the partners."

"Not your young man in a hurry here, I hope?"

Tim squirmed and blushed.

"No your honor. It was Thomas Quinn, a long-time associate in our T&E section. Sadly, he died a few weeks ago of a heart attack."

Zaggert reacted first. He seemed truly shocked. "It's Tom Quinn you were talking about? Oh my God. I can't believe it! I've always known him to be such perfect gentleman, an honest man. And a very good attorney."

"Yes, Mr. Zaggert, I agree," said Rem. "I'm finding all of this very shocking and very upsetting. And now Mr. Finley's client Harold Simpson is alleging that Tom coerced him into accepting a settlement, against Mr. Finley's advice. He's claiming Tom threatened to report some criminal acts to the authorities, acts that he falsely suggested would result in a lengthy prison sentence for Mr. Simpson."

Zaggert rallied to Quinn's defense.

"I just don't believe that, Mr. Finley," he said, glancing at the judge. "Mr. Finley, I've observed your client during some of the depositions, and I can't imagine he's as unsophisticated in that area as this accusation would imply."

"I agree wholeheartedly, Jack." Rem resorted to Finley's familiar form of address. He welcomed any ally at this point, even if only for what amounted to damage control. "I don't know what Tom was up to, and I certainly can't excuse it in any event, but I think I knew him well enough to say that he would never have done anything as insidious as that. And to what end? The case was certainly not settled cheaply. We all know that."

Judge DiMalco had apparently heard enough.

"Mr. Watson, I'm afraid I will have to report this matter to the Appellate Division. How they will view Mr. Quinn's conduct, and your firm's responsibility, will be up to them.

As far as this probate proceeding is concerned, however, I would like to speak with Mr. Finley alone, if you have no objection."

"None whatsoever, your honor. Mr. O'Leary and I will wait outside."

"Fine. We'll let you know when we need you. Jack, why don't you stay? And please shut the door after these gentlemen leave, would you?"

Watson and Tim rose from their seats and left the room. They passed through the anteroom and stepped into the corridor. Watson was visibly upset.

"That Finley is a real piece of work. He can't possibly believe that story of Harold's, assuming it is Harold's. I think the 'gist' has been amply embroidered on its way to our ears. We'd better let Greg and poor Ted know what's going on. I should stay here. Would you go find them and bring them back?"

"Sure. I'll be back in a minute."

Where the heck was Marge?

45

TIM FOUND BRACKEN standing nervously near the bank of pay phones at the end of the corridor. Trout was on the telephone in one of the booths. He hung up when he saw Tim.

"What's going on, Tim? I thought we were here to put the settlement on the record. I've got a lunch date at noon."

"I'll let Rem tell you, Greg. It's complicated."

When they rejoined Watson, he filled them in and apologized to Trout for the delay, but told him he might want to consider canceling his lunch date.

"Really, Rem, is that absolutely necessary? This is one of the bank's major relationships I'm meeting with."

"Greg, I'm very sorry, but judges don't take kindly to litigants leaving the courthouse in the middle of something like this because of their lunch plans. Maybe someone else from your shop can cover for you."

"But Rem, we're lunching at Delmonico's. It's a wonderful restaurant and the client is very special as well. Can't you patch me in by telephone? I'm sure the headwaiter would make a phone available to me."

"No I can't, Greg, That's impossible."

Sighing with annoyance, Trout went back to the pay phones to cancel his lunch plans.

10 minutes had passed when the judge's law secretary came out into the hallway and called Harold Simpson's name. Harold, who had been standing by himself and scrutinizing what appeared to be the Daily Racing Form, looked up.

"That's me."

"Would you please come inside, Mr. Simpson?"

Harold folded the Racing Form and tucked it under his arm as he brushed past them on his way toward the judge's chambers, giving them one of his more triumphant smirks as he went by.

Fifteen minutes passed before Michael Finley, looking fierce, and Harold Simpson, still smirking and clearly not concerned about criminal prosecution and lengthy prison terms, exited the anteroom. They were followed closely by Jack Zaggert, who beckoned to Watson.

"The judge would like to speak to you, Mr. Watson," he said. "Please bring only your associate. Clients should stay outside."

Rem and Tim followed him back into the judge's chambers. "Gentlemen," said Judge DiMalco. "Mr. Finley and I had a little heart-to-heart and then I asked him to bring his client in. I thought Mr. Simpson should be present for what I had to say. Basically, I told them that no matter how serious the improper contact may have been, I was having a very hard time accepting Harold's version of his calls from your deceased associate. An extortionist gets something in return for his efforts. Quinn wouldn't have shared in Mr. Bracken's receiving a greater portion of the estate, even if Bracken were your client, unless Quinn was a partner in your firm and you were handling this case on a contingency. He wasn't a partner, and I assume you're not working on a contingency, anyway. Am I right?"

"Absolutely, your honor. We're working on an hourly basis, as usual. And you're also right in assuming that Tom

Quinn did not share in the firm's profits. He was a salaried employee."

"So, then, Mr. Watson, here's what I would suggest. You'll have to suffer a little bit for what happened here, so I think you should be willing to increase the settlement to thirty-three million dollars. Actually, I tried to get Mr. Finley to go along with thirty-two million, but he insisted on the thirty-three. I think we both know why—the arithmetic is simpler."

A little smile passed briefly over the judge's lips, and then he resumed.

"You may want to make up some of the extra three million to Mr. Bracken, but that's up to you and your firm."

Tim noticed Rem grimace ever so slightly.

"In any case this is a lot less than the forty-five million Mr. Finley was demanding, and he also agreed not to publicize the ethical issue, at least until the Appellate Division's review has run its course. That's essentially it. I thought I should speak to you first without your client being present, but why don't you go talk to him and to Mr. Bracken's attorney now and let's see if we can wrap this up?"

"All right, your honor. I will," said Rem. "As Mr. Zaggert knows, the Grant Pivens firm has counseled Mr. Bracken with respect to the thirty million dollar settlement, and has authorized us to appear for him today and to join in that settlement on his behalf. I'll have to call Wally Denton over there to alert him to these new developments, but that should not be a problem. He said he would be standing by if we needed to speak with him this morning."

"Fine, Mr. Watson. Why don't you do that, and then let Mr. Zaggert know when you're ready to speak with me again."

"I will, your honor. Thank you for your help."

The two men left the judge's chambers and continued on to the corridor, where they found an annoyed Greg Trout and a very pale Ted Bracken. Rem gestured them to the far end of the corridor, out of earshot of Finley and Harold. When they were far enough away to speak without being overheard, he described his conversation with the judge. Trout said he thought the whole thing was a travesty, although he seemed anxious to conclude matters and get to lunch, which he had apparently pushed back an hour rather than cancelled.

"What choice do we have, Rem? Pay them their blood money and send them back to their rat holes. I dread dealing with them, but what can we do?"

Watson turned to Bracken.

"Ted, how do you feel about this? After taxes, you'll only get about eight million. A lot less than the twenty-five million dollars Rex wanted you to have."

"Mr. Watson, I just want this to end. Pay them whatever they want. I don't even know what to do with eight million dollars, let alone three times that much."

"I'm sorry we couldn't have done better for you. Let's give Wally Denton a call so you can have the benefit of his advice."

Rem reached into one of the phone booths, took the phone from its cradle and dialed Denton's direct line. He got him on the second ring, described the new developments, and handed the phone to Ted Bracken. Bracken's hand was trembling as took it.

The conversation was brief. Denton reminded Bracken of his trust in Rem's professional judgment, and said that if Watson felt that this was the best he could do under the circumstances, Bracken should accept the new terms. He did note the possibility of some reduction of Bradford, Lord and Turner's fee in light of the judge's comment, but said that could be worked out later. Bracken once again said he just wanted the whole thing to be over, and they agreed that he should go forward. Rem got back on the phone with Denton, thanked him for his help, and grimly said he would be in touch about the "fee matter."

As soon as he ended the call, Watson told Tim to come

with him and they went back to see the judge. After learning of their willingness to accept the revised settlement terms, Surrogate DiMalco asked them to bring in the bank officer and the beneficiary. When all were present, he thanked them, said that a lost Will case is almost impossible to win and that taking the settlement, however difficult it might be under the circumstances, was in everyone's best interest. Speaking directly to Ted Bracken, he said, "You'll still receive a very substantial sum of money, and if you went to trial you might have gotten nothing." He then instructed them to wait outside until the case was called again. He would meet them in the courtroom shortly after that.

Best interest or not, it was hard for any of them, other than Greg Trout, not to feel like mourners approaching the funeral home as they filed out of DiMalco's chambers and walked toward the courtroom doors.

A few minutes later, Jack Zaggert appeared in the corridor. "Would the parties and counsel please go into the courtroom? The surrogate would like to have the stipulation of settlement in the Simpson matter placed on the record and to take the parties' consents at this time."

Rem, Trout, Bracken and Tim started toward the courtroom. Mickey Finley and Harold Simpson did the same.

46

THEY ENTERED THE COURTROOM and sat at the two tables indicated by Zaggert, one for Watson's group and the other for Finley and his client. Tim, still seeing no sign of Marge, realized that his last gasp effort to save the case had been a failure.

"All rise!" shouted the court attendant. They all got to their feet as Judge DiMalco came into the courtroom and stepped up to the bench. He addressed them.

"Please be seated. The court reporter will take the appearances of the parties and their attorneys. Mr. Malone?"

A gentleman seated below the judge's bench turned to them and began tapping on his stenotype machine as they identified themselves. When he was finished, he looked up at the judge. "I have them, your honor."

"Thank you, Mr. Malone. All right, let the record show that a settlement of the objections filed in the probate proceeding in the Estate of Reginald V. Simpson has been reached. I understand that Mr. Watson, who has acted as counsel for the proponent in this proceeding, wishes to read the terms of the settlement into the record at this time, after which the parties will be asked to state their understanding of the settlement and their agreement to be bound by it. Mr. Watson?"

"Thank you, your honor. The Will of Reginald V. Simpson, dated July 17, 1968, a copy of which has been offered for probate in this proceeding, and to which objections have been filed—"

"Judge, I'm sorry." A small grey-haired woman had entered the courtroom from the door leading to the judge's chambers.

Judge DiMalco looked startled, as did Rem. "Irma? We're putting a stipulation on the record."

"I know, judge, but there's a woman on the phone. She said it was urgent, and that it related to the Simpson case."

"A woman? Did she at least give her name?"

"Yes, judge. She said her name was Margery Conley and that she was calling from the Suffolk County Surrogate's Court. She also said she was working with one of the attorneys in this case. A Timothy O'Leary."

Rem looked angrily toward Tim, and then turned back to the surrogate.

"I apologize, your honor. I will speak to Mr. O'Leary about this after we finish here. May I continue?"

"Not yet, Mr. Watson. Let me hear from Mr. O'Leary first. Mr. O'Leary, do you know what this is about?"

There was no turning back now. "Yes I do, your honor. I think we should hear what she has to say. I think it will bear on the parties' willingness to enter into the settlement."

"All right, young man, but this is very irregular. I hope for your sake it isn't frivolous. My secretary will show you where you can take the call. I'll give you two minutes. No more."

Tim followed Irma into the judge's chambers. She pointed to the phone lying on the desk. He picked it up.

"Marge?"

"Don't settle, Tim. It's here!"

"Marge, give me some details. Quick! They're already in

the courtroom." He stood there listening to her for about 30 seconds.

"I'll call you back Marge. I've got to stop them. Bye." Tim raced for the door.

Back in the courtroom, he walked quickly to where Watson, looking embarrassed, was still standing.

"Rem." He whispered, "I know where the Will is!"

This got Watson's attention.

"What? Whose Will? Rex Simpson? This better not be a joke. Where is it?"

Tim thought that it was amazing what people will say when they're stunned, and Watson was stunned, or he never would have considered a statement like this at a time like this and in a place like this, or from a person in Tim's currently precarious position, to be a joke, but at least Tim had his attention.

"Rex Simpson's Will is on file in the Suffolk County Surrogate's Court in Riverhead out on Long Island. Tom Quinn filed it there."

"Are you sure?"

"I am. I hope you understand, but when I finally figured it out last night, it was too late to do anything other than ask my friend the private investigator to go out there this morning and check. I couldn't be a hundred percent sure until she did, and there was no time to send someone from the office. I called her in the middle of the night and asked her to go. I'm sorry. I know how you feel about my involving her in the case, but I just felt I had no choice."

"We'll worry about that later. You're sure this is his Will?"

"Ninety-nine percent sure, Rem."

"Ninety-nine percent? What does that mean?"

"Well, Marge spoke to the clerk, and confirmed there was a Will for Reginald Simpson on file for safekeeping. The address given by the person who filed it matches Rex's East Hampton address. The filing date is the same as the date on Tom Quinn's three dollar check to the clerk that Tom's wife showed me, and also the date of the receipt referred to in Tom's notes. The only problem is that the clerk wouldn't show the Will to Marge, because she's not the attorney who filed it, or from his office. And she didn't even have a death certificate with her to prove Rex Simpson had died."

"What about the date of the Will?"

"The clerk told her he didn't know the date."

"Are we ready to proceed, you two?" The judge was glaring down from the bench.

"Rem, we can't go forward. It's not right!"

"It's okay, Tim. Sit. I'll take it from here." Rem for once looked kindly at Tim, then turned to the judge as Tim sank into the chair behind him.

"Your honor, we have a development here that may be of great significance. May I approach the bench?"

"Please." Impatient but curious, he motioned the attorneys forward. When they arrived at the bench, he leaned forward expectantly.

"What's this all about, Mr. Watson?"

"Your honor, I think we may have found the missing Will."

"You think?"

"Yeah. What kind of game are you playing now, Watson?" Finley, despite his usual gruff manner, looked worried. "Let's get this stipulation on the record and get the show on the road."

Rem ignored the interruption and pressed on. "We have just learned that a Will of Reginald Simpson, our decedent, was filed for safekeeping, probably by Mr. Quinn, in the Suffolk County Surrogate's Court on August seventh of last year. We don't yet know for sure that it is the missing last Will, but we are fairly certain that it is. The clerk in Suffolk will not remove it from its sealed wrapper and disclose its contents, however, because our representative is not authorized under the statute to see it. We need your help."

Our representative? A battlefield commission? Tim liked

what he was hearing.

"All right, Mr. Watson, let me make a call. Everyone stay here. I'll be right back." Judge DiMalco left the courtroom through the side door to his chambers.

Within a few minutes he was back.

"I just spoke with Surrogate Hildreth out in Riverhead. He ordered his clerk to open the sealed wrapper, remove the Will and call me. I should hear from him shortly. In the meantime, I want you all to stay here. Except you, Mr. Malone. I want you to come with me. And bring your stenotype machine."

The tension, which had been growing since the news of the possible discovery of the Will, was now reaching the breaking point. Even Trout's lunch plans seemed to have taken a back seat. Tim assumed he was moving Ted to the top of his list of potential "special" clients, considering the sudden prospect of an exponential increase in Ted's investable assets. Watson told Tim he was keeping his fingers crossed. Finley told Harold to "just shut up" when Harold started telling him that a deal was a deal and they shouldn't be able to change it now. Any visions of an owner's box at next year's Kentucky Derby were suddenly up in the air.

"All right, everyone take your seats." The judge was back. "The Will on file in the Suffolk Surrogate's Court appears to be the missing original of the Will that has been offered for probate in this proceeding. Relevant portions of the Will have been read to me over the phone. The phone's speaker was turned on, so Mr. Malone could hear and transcribe my conversation with Surrogate Hildreth's law secretary. Mr. Malone, would you be kind enough to read back what you transcribed?"

The first provision Malone read told everyone what they needed to know.

"Fifth: I make no provision for my brother Harold Simpson, for reasons well known to him."

The other provisions, appointing the family trusts in Ted

Bracken's favor, giving all of Rex's own assets to Ted, and appointing Morgan Guaranty as executor, were just icing on the cake. The lost Will had been found!

Rem rose to his feet. "Your honor, I think it is fair to say that the settlement agreement we reached earlier today is no longer acceptable to Mr. Bracken or to the petitioner Morgan Guaranty, which has a statutory duty to see that a valid last Will naming it as executor is admitted to probate and its provisions faithfully adhered to. This being Reginald Simpson's valid last Will, I would ask that your honor sign an order, which we will prepare and submit to you, directing the transmittal of the Will to this court, after which I intend to move for summary judgment admitting it to probate and appointing Morgan Guaranty executor to execute its provisions."

The judge turned to Finley. "Mr. Finley, would you like to reply?"

"I feel like I've been sucker punched, judge. Maybe Mr. Watson and I should talk."

"Very well, gentlemen. We will adjourn for today. Please be here tomorrow morning at 9:30 to let me know whether I can be of any further assistance. Otherwise I will give Mr. Watson time to submit his order and make his motion."

The judge rose and left the courtroom. Rem told Tim he had done a "fine job" and was a credit to the firm. Greg Trout congratulated him, and Ted Bracken shook his hand, got choked up, and managed simply to say, "Thank you." That was more than enough for Tim—he was a lawyer now.

"Rem, I need to talk to you." It was Mickey Finley, now adopting the more familiar first name form of address that had eluded him before. He actually seemed friendly, unlike his client, who was stalking around the courtroom, muttering something about Tom Quinn being a certain part of the human anatomy.

"No hard feelings, Rem. Crazy how these things turn out, isn't it? Hey, I could've had that kid O'Leary, you know. You oughta thank me for letting him go."

"Letting me—" Tim wasn't even able to get a sentence in.

"Listen, there's always a chance we can beat your summary judgment motion and get this case to trial," Finley went on. "Then who knows? A jury can come up with the wildest verdicts. Maybe we can wrap this up on consent today. How about throwing a bone to my client, say ten percent? I always say I'll give ten percent to anyone to get rid of them. How about it?"

"Mickey, no. You've got nothing here now. Why should I give away Mr. Bracken's money? You have no chance of defeating the motion. Our only weakness was that we couldn't find the Will. That's all changed now."

"Wait, Mr. Watson. Could I speak with you, please?" Bracken had come over to the two lawyers when he heard what was being said.

"Sure, Ted, why don't we step over there for a moment? Excuse me, Mickey."

Tim saw a surprised expression come over Rem's face as Bracken spoke to him. Finally, he nodded and returned to where Finley was standing.

"Mickey, Mr. Bracken is a good man. He is saddened by the fact your client and his brother were estranged for so many years, and he feels that Harold should receive something from the estate. He has authorized me to settle your probate objections for one million dollars."

"Could you make it one point five?"

"Let me talk to him. I'll see what I can do."

Watson went over to Bracken and explained the "divisible by three" rule, with which he was now familiar. Bracken said Mr. Finley had obviously worked very hard for his client, and it would be a shame if he received nothing for all of his efforts. Watson told Bracken that he was misunderstanding what they were talking about, that Mr. Finley would be paid in any event, albeit a bit less and not a round amount. Bracken smiled indulgently and said "I'm just pulling your leg, Mr. Watson. Where I come from, lawyers always take a third of whatever they get for you. One million five is fine. Let's all go home."

And so ended the contested probate proceeding in the Estate of Reginald V. Simpson, late of the County of New York. Or was it the County of Suffolk? Only time and the New York City tax collector would tell.

— EPILOGUE —

TED BRACKEN PROVED to be a generous man. He became very friendly with Tim after the case was over, and learned of the plight of Quinn's two grandchildren. Tim arranged for him to meet with them at one of Kitty Quinn's Happy Hours, at which he contented himself with a beer, politely declining Kitty's offer of one of her blue martinis. Afterwards, Ted declared that he would pay the costs of Kevin's last year at Xaverian High School, and all of Kevin and Megan's college expenses. He also purchased an annuity for Kitty which would pay her $75,000 per year for the rest of her life, saying that it was clear to him that Tom Quinn had done what he did only to help her and "the kids." Furthermore, it was obvious to him that Tom had gone into the office on a Sunday and opened the Simpson folder because he had decided he couldn't go through with his scheme, and was preparing to make a clean breast of it to Rem Watson the following morning.

Ken Clark, although skeptical about Tom's last minute change of heart, was sure he knew why Tom had chosen to file the Will in the Suffolk County Surrogate's Court, rather than keeping it at home or in the office or in a safe deposit box. Rex Simpson's Will would have been a lot harder to explain than a spare telephone in his desk drawer, if Kitty Quinn happened to come across it, and a bill for rental of a new safe deposit box on which she had not been named deputy would have really caused a firestorm. The office? What if Tom was out sick and someone went looking for something in his desk? Much too risky. But Tom knew better than anyone that no one ever looks in the "Poor Man's Will Safe." Not even that clerk who told Tim the court always checks, Ken suspected. But just to be sure, Tom must have come up with the Suffolk idea, which was, Ken admitted, brilliant. At any time along the way, an anonymous call to Rem Watson disclosing the Will's hiding place could have blown a Harold double-cross out of the water. But if the plan had succeeded and Tom got his "payday," the Will would have gathered dust in Suffolk until that archeologist writing his doctoral thesis found it a few thousand years later.

Harold Simpson took the one million that was left for him after Mickey Finley's $500,000 contingent fee and, after giving $50,000 to Sister Jeanne at Our Lady of Perpetual Help, gradually lost the remaining 950 grand over the next three years at various racetracks around the country. He then applied for unemployment benefits, but withdrew his application when he was told he would have to interview for various job openings that involved manual labor in order to continue to qualify for assistance. He never forgave Quinn for not destroying the Will as he had promised.

Finley took his half a million dollar fee and used some of it to place ads in the New York Post and the Daily News, defying the rules against lawyer advertising which would not be overturned for almost a decade. He trumpeted his qualifications as a specialist in all forms of estate litigation, promising to break the grip of the "Big Wall Street Boys" on "your rightful inheritance." Free consultations, of course.

Greg Trout continued to work at Morgan Guaranty Trust Company, until he accepted an early retirement package in a corporate downsizing a few years after the litigation ended. He missed the lunch at Delmonico's on the day the case was closed, and never had another opportunity to dine there, at least not at the bank's expense.

The ethics inquiry never became intense, primarily because the principal offender was deceased. The panel issued a mild rebuke to Bradford, Lord and Turner for failure to regularly warn its associates of the ethical rules governing the practice of law. It acknowledged, however, that Quinn was well aware of those rules, since he had lectured frequently at seminars sponsored by the Association of the Bar of the City of New York on many topics relating to estate planning and administration, and the ethical standards expected of attorneys in matters involving estates and trusts, including litigated matters.

Tim was of course wholeheartedly forgiven for his unauthorized use of an outside investigator, but was gently asked to "go through channels" before doing so again in the future. His prospects at Bradford, Lord and Turner went from glum to rosy overnight, and he was described by Austin Chamberlain as "a young man of spirit and determination, in the finest traditions of the firm, an example to those who would sully the name of the profession with their deceitful practices," an obvious reference to the infamous Mickey Finn.

Marge gave up smoking for good, but was still a regular patron at Smokey's, which somehow retained its right to operate as a tobacco bar when anti-smoking laws were enacted in later years. Rem was sufficiently impressed with her work on the Simpson case that he referred several of his partners to her on other matters.

Tim's roommate Rick continued his hitchhiking trip around the country, until he happened upon the Blackfoot Indian Reservation in Montana. There he became enamored of the plight of those Indians and of the descendants of Chief

Joseph of the Nez Perce tribe, got himself admitted to the Montana Bar, and became a successful advocate for Indian rights, to the perpetual annoyance of the local ranchers. He invited Tim to join him. Tim thanked him for the offer, but said he had already made plans with a new roommate.

Tim and Marge were married two years after the case ended. Shirley, still the only waitress at Smokey's and still called "Toots" by its regulars, was Marge's matron of honor. Ted Bracken was Tim's best man. Ken Clark, appalled that the reception was to be held at Smokey's, refused to attend, but agreed to at least go to the church service beforehand, insisting that he be the one to select the music for the ceremony. Tim consented, but only on condition that any Bach selection be limited to no more than five minutes in duration. Tim's father and two sisters attended, of course. All three cried when Mr. O'Leary put his arms around his daughters' shoulders and said, "Your mother, may she rest in peace, would have been so very proud of the three of you."

On the altar, Marge whispered to Tim, "Tim, what were the three wishes you made in church that day we went to Tom Quinn's funeral?"

"I still can't tell you, Marge. Those are the rules. But they all came true."

"So did mine, Tim, so did mine."

www.ingramcontent.com/pod-product-compliance
Lightning Source LLC
Chambersburg PA
CBHW071130170626
46809CB00002B/557